THE EARLY EDUCATION LEADER'S GUIDE

Also from Nonie K. Lesaux

Making Assessment Matter:
Using Test Results to Differentiate Reading Instruction
Nonie K. Lesaux and Sky H. Marietta

Teaching Advanced Literacy Skills:
A Guide for Leaders in Linguistically Diverse Schools
*Nonie K. Lesaux, Emily Phillips Galloway,
and Sky H. Marietta*

The Early Education Leader's Guide

Program Leadership and Professional Learning for the 21st Century

Nonie K. Lesaux
Stephanie M. Jones
Annie Connors
Robin Kane

THE GUILFORD PRESS
New York   London

Library of Congress Cataloging-in-Publication Data is available from the publisher.

978-1-4625-3751-8 (paperback)
978-1-4625-3752-5 (hardcover)

About the Authors

Nonie K. Lesaux, PhD, is Academic Dean and the Juliana W. and William Foss Thompson Professor of Education and Society at the Harvard Graduate School of Education. She leads a research program guided by the goal of increasing opportunities to learn for children and youth from diverse linguistic, cultural, and economic backgrounds. She has served on the Institute of Medicine and National Research Council's Committee on the Science of Children Birth to Age 8, and currently serves as Chair of the Massachusetts Board of Early Education and Care. With Stephanie M. Jones, Dr. Lesaux directs the Saul Zaentz Early Education Initiative at the Harvard Graduate School of Education.

Stephanie M. Jones, PhD, is Professor of Education at the Harvard Graduate School of Education. Anchored in prevention science, her research focuses on the effects of poverty and exposure to violence on the social, emotional, and behavioral development of children and youth. She has conducted numerous evaluations of programs and early education efforts, including the Head Start CARES initiative. She is a recipient of the Grawemeyer Award in Education for her work with Edward Zigler and Walter S. Gilliam on *A Vision for Universal Preschool Education*. With Nonie K. Lesaux, Dr. Jones directs the Saul Zaentz Early Education Initiative at the Harvard Graduate School of Education.

Annie Connors, MEd, is a practitioner with over a decade of primary teaching experience in public schools. A literacy specialist and reading coach in the Greater Boston area, specializing in providing direct instruction to students and professional development for educators, Ms. Connors has served as a literacy consultant to education publishers and research groups on a variety of programs and initiatives.

Robin Kane is Assistant Director of Professional Institutes and Partnerships at the Saul Zaentz Early Education Initiative at the Harvard Graduate School of Education. She provides professional development training and coaching to novice and experienced early educators. Most recently, she has worked on the development of early literacy curricula and interventions for an urban school district, and the design and implementation of innovative professional development programs for early education leaders. Ms. Kane founded a child development center in 1991, where she taught children and mentored teachers for over 23 years.

Acknowledgments

With the pressing need for improved and expanded formal learning opportunities for all children, it's a new world for early education. States, communities, and school districts are working on prekindergarten plans and birth to third-grade pathways, and they are looking, in particular, to science that is based on research–practice partnerships for guidance.

Our inspiration for this book grew out of today's landscape and a multi-year collaboration—one in which we designed an approach to building early educators' core competencies that research tells us are crucial for creating learning environments and opportunities that promote early learning and development. In this partnership, we came to understand the challenges of, and see the possibilities for, supporting the adults who are charged with—and central to—everyday learning and development, and what this means for effective leadership in early education.

As this book goes to press, there are many individuals to thank for their collaboration and partnership in this collective effort. Julie Russ Harris was instrumental to this work for several years; in participating centers, she was a respected facilitator and a close observer of young children and the nuances of daily practice. In our research group, she led much of our research that investigated adult practice in relation to children's early learning and development and worked on earlier versions of this manuscript. Rebecca Givens Rolland played a similar role in the earliest years as a trusted facilitator and researcher. Laura Mendes, in the Springfield Public Schools, has been a thought partner in the field for several years. We also thank the many center directors and teachers with whom we have had the opportunity to collaborate. At the Harvard Graduate School of Education, we have the privilege of learning from a tremendous group of colleagues in the Language Diversity and Literacy Development research group and in the EASEL Lab. We thank each of them for their collaboration that fuels our thinking and work.

Finally, we thank MG Prezioso for her work in preparing the manuscript for publication, and also Craig Thomas, Senior Editor at The Guilford Press, for his investment in the ideas presented here. In closing, we dedicate this book to the many young children and their teachers who have inspired us along the way.

We wrote *The Early Education Leader's Guide* to give today's program leaders and staff developers a road map for designing and implementing engaging approaches to professional development and coaching. As a complement to this book, we have created a website that provides a variety of supplemental resources, including planning tools, checklists, protocols, self-study materials, and more. Grounded in the science that lays the foundation for the book, these resources are designed to support leaders to turn their planning into action and are available at *https://zaentz.gse.harvard.edu/leaders-book-resources*.

Contents

PART III. Conclusion

Purchasers of this book can download and print enlarged
versions of select figures at *www.guilford.com/lesaux3-forms*
for personal use (see copyright page for details).

CHAPTER 1

Introduction

An Early Educator for the 21st Century

Melinda, the director of the Explorations Early Learning Center, pokes her head into the PreK room during one of her morning walk-throughs of the Center. She sees Jada, a second-year teacher, greeting children and helping them pull off their hats and mittens. The classroom is already abuzz with chatter and movement. Melinda is reminded of last week's Professional Learning Community meeting, where Jada had verbally expressed some frustration over implementing the new changes in the curriculum. "I wonder how Jada is doing," Melinda thinks to herself. "I know she has been struggling with managing her son's asthma. She looks tired." As Melinda looks around and takes in the activity in the room, she pauses and considers Jada's class this year; she has a group that feels especially "young," with several children exhibiting consistently challenging behaviors. Jada is also only in her second year of teaching, still learning about effective management strategies. Melinda greets Jada with a smile and a wave. Jada ekes out a smile and says, "Good morning!" as children tumble out of their coats toward the breakfast awaiting them. "What can I do to better support the teaching and learning in this room?" Melinda wonders, as she steps out to greet the next classroom of children and educators.

Today's early education classroom is a busy and bustling place. Like Melinda at the Explorations Early Learning Center, early education leaders across the nation strive to improve the learning experiences at their sites. They make daily leadership decisions that influence the extent to which children are provided high-quality learning opportunities and experiences. They are responsible for creating a setting that fosters the development of cognitive, emotional, and relational skills. But early education leaders also have a significant responsibility to attend to the educators, like Jada and her colleagues, in these dynamic real-life settings. In fact, their decisions aimed at promoting children's healthy development often have the potential to likewise promote the professional skills and competencies of the early educator. When supported by core knowledge about the science of adult and child learning and a robust understanding of what makes for a high-quality learning environment, the daily leadership decisions made by Melinda and her peers across the nation can support enhanced professional knowledge and develop the capacity among educators and teaching teams to produce teaching and learning that leads to positive outcomes. Melinda and her peers—today's early education leaders—find themselves navigating their professional work in the context of dramatic changes over the last several decades.

In this chapter, we examine these changes, synthesizing both the changes in our early childhood populations and emerging research on the importance of early education and care for today's children and families. We consider the complexity of the early educator role, and we maintain that, especially in light of recent policy changes and the increasing expectations placed on these educators, the field will only improve *if we consider their professional needs as an essential part of any leadership or reform strategy.* In other words, achieving higher-quality learning environments for children means developing educator capacity—genuinely attending to the adults' skills and knowledge. We close the chapter by explaining our work and our approach to professional learning for the 21st-century early educator, along the way providing a road map to guide your reading.

What Is Today's Landscape of Early Education and Care?

The concept and purpose of early education and care has shifted tremendously from when it was first brought to the national stage. Stemming from the need to provide nonparental care for young children during the Great Depression and World War II, early programs provided options for our most impoverished and socioeconomically vulnerable children (Phillips, 2016). As part of the War on Poverty's effort to provide an early boost for at-risk children, Head Start was established in the 1960s. Since then, substantial growth in the number of families with two working parents has driven a much greater need for child care across all income levels, and the number of children in early education and care settings has increased exponentially. Today, 6 out of every 10 children in America attend some type of early education program (U.S. Department of Education, 2015).

Over the last decade, with federal support, the nation has begun to reconsider the traditional model of child care, coming to view it as early education—a means of developing children's minds and their capacities for learning. This shift in perspective is due in part to a dramatic expansion in the science of early learning and development; research focusing on the cognitive, social, and emotional development of young children has identified the long-term positive impacts of high-quality early education, highlighting the importance of these experiences at this critical stage of development (Barnett, 1995; National Association for the Education of Young Children, 2017). The new conceptualization of the model corresponds as well with an emerging science of stress and adversity and with demographic changes in the childhood population. That is, today's young children are more linguistically, culturally, and racially diverse than ever before. They are also faced with challenges that have lasting negative effects on their learning and growth (Brooks-Gunn & Duncan, 1997). For example, it is estimated that nearly 45% of children younger than 5 currently live in low-income households (Grant, Gracy, Goldsmith, Shapiro, & Redlener, 2013), and across all income levels, one in four children experience some type of significant adverse experience (e.g., parental divorce/separation, emotional or physical neglect or abuse). Consequently, access to high-quality early education has been shown to be a key strategy for buffering the effects of stress and adversity, ultimately better preparing all children, even the most vulnerable, for future success in school and life.

In response to these research insights and population changes, federal, state, and community agencies across the nation have ambitiously expanded public options for early education. States, cities, and towns nationwide are actively planning their early education and care strategies, even as conversations about universal prekindergarten abound.

This increased attention to early education represents significant opportunities and substantial challenges. Perhaps the most important challenge is that while access to the early education system is expanding, there is also a need for improvements in quality. For example, returning to the statistic that approximately 6 out of 10 children attend some type of early education program, we note only two or three of those six children attend a high-quality program (Barnett & Nores, 2012). In effect, today's challenge is to improve the quality of early education programs even as access to them continues to grow. After all, it is more than just *access* that counts; the body of evidence underscores that the *quality* of early learning environments, whether within the home, school, or community, and the relationships that are created in these environments, are fundamental to nurturing a healthy child (Carlock, 2011; Jennings & Greenberg, 2009; Jones, Bouffard, & Weissbourd, 2013; Maurer & Brackett, 2004; Roeser, Skinner, Beers & Jennings, 2012).

What Are the Features
of High-Quality Early Learning Environments?

As we anticipate that improvements in these programs will be achieved at scale, how, exactly, do we describe high-quality early learning environments? Well, we understand them to be calm, predictable settings with established routines, where young children regularly engage in rich, stimulating learning experiences that promote cognitive development while building social and emotional skills. And we know that underlying all of them are warm, responsive adult–child relationships. In essence, high-quality learning environments share two fundamental characteristics. First, the environment is *rigorous*. There is a focus on stimulating and accumulating learning experiences that actively build and develop cognitive and social–emotional skills. Children are engaged in activities that center on developing understanding and language simultaneously. And second, the environment is *regulated*. It is routine oriented and predictable; it centers on the flexible, but consistent use of routines, appropriate setting of limits, and warm, responsive adult–child relationships.

In using the terms *rigorous* and *regulated*, we believe we are afforded an opportunity and a necessity to refine—or even redefine—what rigorous means in early education. We would challenge the assumption that "rigor" is synonymous with academics or an academic focus at the expense of the opportunity for discovery and exploration, and we would likewise suggest that all children deserve exposure to academic concepts and ideas in their learning environment. At its core, a rigorous early learning setting is one that engages children with stimulating content that grows over time into accumulated knowledge. In this environment, children are developing their social–emotional and academic competencies *simultaneously,* and educators are supporting them with instructional practices that are deliberately integrated.

This concept of an integrated approach to educating young children is not new to early education leaders and teachers. While many early education settings have long espoused the need to develop the whole child, there are two ways in which the field continues to fall short in implementation. First, in the typical classroom, there tend to be solid lessons and activities throughout the day that aim to build key skills. But these are often independent of one another; in other words, a lot of instruction is happening, but the lessons aren't aligned and don't *add up* to deep learning around a given topic. These lessons and activities are not sufficiently connected and integrated to transform children's development. For example, a classroom might focus for 20 minutes on a numeracy skill and then switch to a play-based activity, like the drama center, and then later engage in story time on the carpet. Each of these activities is important in and of itself, but without a clear through-line between them there are missed opportunities. Second, as also becomes clear, the instructional design is such that the goal of each lesson or activity is most often linked to a single developmental domain, such as language, literacy, and/ or social–emotional competencies.

What is becoming clearer from research, however, is that within our children, each area of development influences the other in profound and even unexpected ways; the evidence shows that social, emotional, cognitive, and linguistic skills and competencies are intertwined in the brain and in behavior, and that interventions focused on integration show stronger effects than those targeting a single area. Therefore, while we vshould ensure that children have an opportunity to experience many different kinds of activities and lessons, the classroom scenario we have just described does not get us to the rigor that is needed and consistent with what we know from the latest findings about early learning, nor does latching on to fads like "academic-oriented" or "play-based" programs. Simply put, it is not enough to just make time for academics and social–emotional learning; understanding the core processes at work for children means embedding elements of these developmental domains within all learning.

What does this look like in a rigorous early learning classroom—where the competency building in the developmental domains is not only connected, but more important, *integrated*? While we address this question in detail in the chapters that follow, for now, imagine a classroom where the goals are to provide direct instruction and intensive support to strengthen literacy skills (e.g., vocabulary) and social–emotional competencies (e.g., emotion management, social skills). To support these goals, the educator creates a curriculum with units of study that are organized around a big idea (e.g., "the world around us") and that include detailed plans for the unit and for its specific lessons—and there are text sets that match the units of study. Integration is achieved when these rich texts (and their corresponding lesson goals) become a platform for discussing academic concepts and the ideas that arise from open-ended questions *and* from promoting language development, self-reflection, and empathy. Lessons are organized around these dual goals. For example, the educator comes prepared with open-ended questions to ask the children so that they explore the book's world, consider the alternative perspectives of the characters, and reflect on their own feelings. At the same time, she is cultivating children's consciousness of language *and* of their feelings and the feelings of others. Reflecting what we know from research, the underlying processes the educator is using in this scenario include exposing children to rich language, building emotional awareness, and cultivating strong teacher–child relationships, all of which lay the foundation for later learning and development.

Establishing rigorous and regulated environments for our youngest learners rests on the shoulders of our early educators, as well as on the early education leaders who support these adults. Getting to this rigorous, high-quality early learning environment that is validated by the latest science means bolstering core knowledge and competencies among educators of young children and providing them with corresponding tools and structures that lay the foundation. As we look to early education as a foundational strategy for giving all children a strong start, one that boosts their early learning and development, we must focus on the cornerstone of the learning environment—the educator—and in many ways, the central determinant of quality. We turn now to the early educator and consider the complexity of that role within today's landscape. From there, we address what all of this means for effective leadership and improvement efforts.

The Professional Demands on Today's Early Educator

To cultivate and sustain a rigorous, regulated early learning experience, the educator must undertake the daily physical, emotional, and mental labor required to provide a stimulating, engaging, and nurturing environment—all while managing challenging behaviors and responding to unpredictability. Across the nation, policymakers and community leaders, along with children and their families, depend on early educators to deliver on this promise, day after day, year after year.

Specifically, by today's standards, the educator is responsible for providing content-rich learning experiences for children, while supporting the social–emotional development that is foundational to learning, and, in turn, cultivating the positive relationships that serve as the basis for healthy development (Joseph & Strain, 2004). Educators must have the tools to model positive behaviors and develop nurturing environments where children feel safe and secure, and where there are routines that give shape to the day's schedule and activities. This is especially challenging given that children this age are only just learning about building relationships and expressing feelings, and are often emotionally turbulent. At the same time, children are physically active, inquisitive, and not yet self-sufficient for many of their basic needs, heightening demands on the adult, who must manage her own emotions and behavior, and maintain calm, as she cultivates a nurturing environment. On a daily basis, drawing on key skills and competencies (as noted parenthetically below), the effective early educator is

- thoughtful about planning but also flexible enough to adjust plans (executive functions);
- emotionally regulated and adaptable in order to adjust her responses to meet challenging situations, and able to model ways to calm down and deescalate (self-regulation strategies);
- attuned to how each child's behavior and development reflects individual

experiences and relates to the child's strengths and weaknesses—while also understanding how adults' and children's behaviors influence one another (emotion awareness and relational skills);

- able to read and understand social cues, manage conflict, and maintain high-quality relationships with children and coworkers (relational skills); and
- able to use talk in intentional and specific ways to promote learning and positive classroom management.

The bottom line is that good teaching places huge demands on the educator in terms of skills and stamina. We might go so far as to say that the early childhood classroom is one of the most taxing professional settings, in the sense of testing the adult's ability to manage her own emotions and behavior. Yet just as the quality of early education programs does not meet our expectations, the quality of our professional development model does not currently match the high expectations we have for these educators. Investments in early educators' professional supports and knowledge, and ultimately working conditions, have not kept pace with their investments in our children, nor have these investments kept pace with what the science of early learning and development and the science of adult learning and of improvement tells us about what is needed.

As we look to early education as a foundational strategy for boosting early learning and development—and as we bear in mind its great potential—we must redouble our efforts to support educators professionally. One way to do this is to focus on key competencies that early educators need in order to cultivate and sustain a high-quality learning environment, meanwhile meeting their daily work challenges and the needs of an increasingly diverse population of children, including those facing stress and adversity. And getting there involves having strong leadership and professional supports—in many respects, a new model of professional development that will support the early educator in ways that are meaningful and lasting.

21st-Century Professional Learning in Early Education: The Inspiration for This Book

In most discussions about improving the quality of early education, and in the designs of many plans and strategies to improve practice, the paradox is this: There is a tendency to skip over the adults and focus overwhelmingly on the children, without considering educator capacity and needs. This is evident in the questions we typically ask: What kind of curriculum would be best for children? What is the right philosophy for classroom management? How do we ensure that we are exposing children to different cultures? What is our plan for maximizing outside time during the winter months? Yet, of course, the success of these plans and decisions depends almost entirely on the educator's skills and competencies to create and sustain the learning environment, while simultaneously implementing and integrating any new specific initiative or program. Therefore, our own approach to improving the quality of practice, drawn from the science of early learning and development and adult learning and development has taken an exclusively adult-focused strategy. Our work recognizes the needs (skills and knowledge) of the educator and responds to these needs with a strategic, meaningful, and competency-based approach to professional development.

The content of this book is informed, in part, by our 3-year collaboration with educators at early education centers in two urban cities. The resulting professional learning program, *The Rigorous and Regulated Learning Environment,* embodies the methods discussed throughout this book. Designed to provide professional learning to early educators that is intensive, collaborative, and directly linked to classroom practice and site-level data, our approach focuses on four key educator competencies: executive functions, emotion regulation, relationship cultivation, and the use of talk for early learning.

The model we used comprised (1) site-based, weekly, 1-hour workshops that involved discussions anchored in case studies, reflective exercises, and the co-construction of professional practices and (2) classroom-based coaching sessions during which educators applied new practices and reflected on their use. By guiding these educators to notice and manage their own executive functions, emotions, and interpersonal relationships, we supported them in becoming more attuned to the learning environment and the reciprocity between their own emotion management and that of the children. Thus they came away with an enhanced understanding of the learning environment as a *system* of relationships and interactions. Additionally, as educators increased their capacities to create positive cycles of classroom interactions, we found that they were more inclined to embrace the professional learning approach. Enthusiastic about their own collaborative, professional work, they then engaged in professional learning communities to continue the discussions, learning from one another, while simultaneously cultivating high-quality early learning experiences and environments for their learners.

Throughout the book, we refer to our experiences working with early educators participating in the approach, and share the tools and strategies we used to develop their capabilities. While the majority of this work has been completed, some of it is ongoing, as we begin to share our learning with stakeholders in a variety of domains. As you read, you will see artifacts of our collaboration with early educators, and we hope that these descriptions and resources help you to link our work with endeavors at your site.

Our Case Setting: The Explorations Early Learning Center

Throughout the book, we visit the Explorations Early Learning Center, which is a fictional place, but a case setting that is grounded in our collective experiences in the early education field, particularly at sites serving high numbers of children facing stress and adversity. In each of the book's chapters, we include an introductory vignette that serves as a springboard for the discussion, as well as a lens through which to view and experience the content. Similar to the vignette at the opening of this chapter, the beginnings of subsequent chapters explore the joys and frustrations experienced in a typical early education setting, taking into account the stress that may come with working closely with other adults in what can often be chaotic circumstances, the energy and planning necessary to be both an early educator and an early education leader, the balancing of behavioral expectations with learning expectations, and the complexity of designing meaningful professional development.

The director of the Explorations Early Learning Center, Melinda, is motivated to invest in the educators at the center and, as a result, engages them in professional development experiences centered on collaboration and the increased use of classroom talk. Like many early education leaders, Melinda gathers and looks for patterns in site-level data to make improvements at the center. Still, she struggles with being an agent of meaningful change, and while she wants to best support the teaching and learning at the center, she experiences both optimism and uncertainty—the latter from being bogged down with daily operations, including compliance and regulation processes. Alongside Melinda, we look into professional moments with Jada, a prekindergarten teacher; Maria, Jada's co-teacher; and Karen, a Professional Learning Community facilitator and coach. The cases are based on actual moments we have witnessed in the field that we hope will provide you with connections to experiences in your own work.

The Book's Road Map

In the chapters that follow, we describe a new approach to professional development and include a set of strategies for improving the quality of early education settings. Written as a guide for leaders in early education—from coaches, to school leaders, to policymakers—this book supports improved teaching and learning in these settings by providing concrete and specific on-the-ground resources. Our intention is to help guide your strategic decision making in a user-friendly way that has the potential to directly help the educators at your site.

As Figure 1.1 shows, the book is organized into two main sections. In Part I, we focus on the adult competencies that are required for cultivating a rich, nurturing, and high-quality early learning environment. We call these competencies *cornerstone educator competencies* because they support educators' success, as well as children's learning and development (see Figure 1.2). If early educators can develop awareness of, monitor, and effectively incorporate aspects of these competencies into their work (through leaders' strategic vision and support for effective professional learning), based on what we know from current research, children's outcomes are very likely to improve.

Each of the chapters in Part I describes and discusses the educator competencies that contribute to prosocial, emotionally supportive, and cognitively stimulating learning environments (see Figure 1.3). We offer tools and

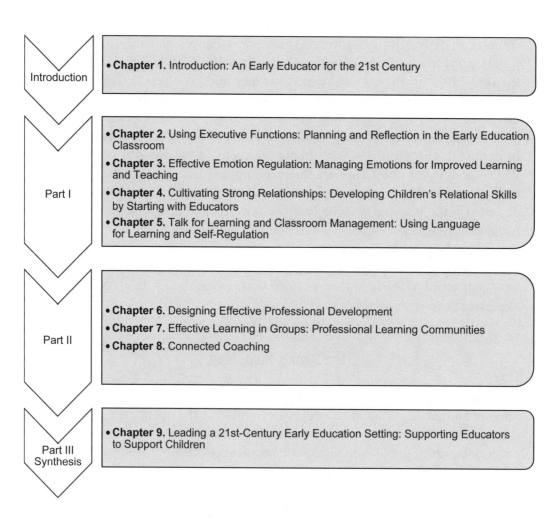

Introduction
- **Chapter 1.** Introduction: An Early Educator for the 21st Century

Part I
- **Chapter 2.** Using Executive Functions: Planning and Reflection in the Early Education Classroom
- **Chapter 3.** Effective Emotion Regulation: Managing Emotions for Improved Learning and Teaching
- **Chapter 4.** Cultivating Strong Relationships: Developing Children's Relational Skills by Starting with Educators
- **Chapter 5.** Talk for Learning and Classroom Management: Using Language for Learning and Self-Regulation

Part II
- **Chapter 6.** Designing Effective Professional Development
- **Chapter 7.** Effective Learning in Groups: Professional Learning Communities
- **Chapter 8.** Connected Coaching

Part III Synthesis
- **Chapter 9.** Leading a 21st-Century Early Education Setting: Supporting Educators to Support Children

FIGURE 1.1. A road map for this book.

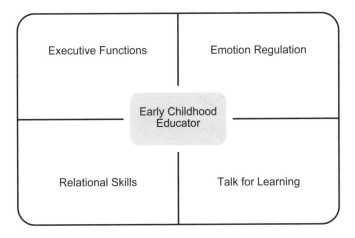

FIGURE 1.2. Early educator competencies discussed in Part I.

strategies to support early educators' use of executive-function strategies (see Chapter 2) and highlight instructional planning and reflection. We discuss what is involved in effective emotion regulation (see Chapter 3), address its impact on teaching and learning, and discuss practical strategies for emotion awareness and emotion management. We then focus on the importance of building strong relationships, starting with professional relationships, by identifying practical strategies for the on-site development of this educator competency (see Chapter 4). Finally, we define and discuss *talk for learning,* a strategy that enhances both early learning and classroom management, and

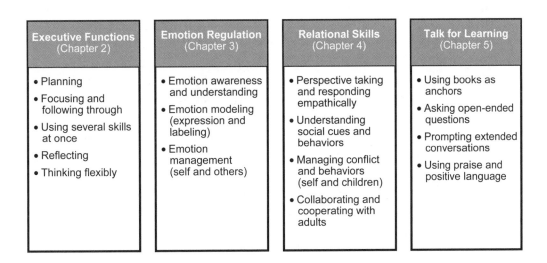

FIGURE 1.3. Early educator competencies outlined by chapter.

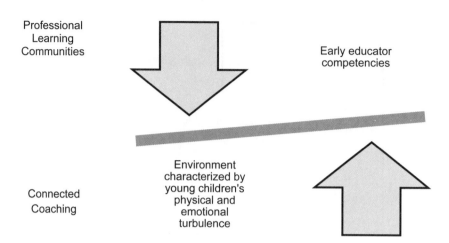

FIGURE 1.4. Promising professional development structures to support the educator within the early education environment, discussed in Part II.

provide strategies for shaping classroom talk to benefit children *and* educators (see Chapter 5).

In Part II, we discuss the ways in which leaders can cultivate these cornerstone educator competencies through professional development. We discuss the need for shifting professional development strategies and structures to encompass a 21st-century model of professional learning, and we consider the formats and approaches that have the highest impact for capacity building (Chapter 6). Included in this approach are two models of professional development: professional learning communities (Chapter 7) and connected coaching (Chapter 8). We also delve into the strategies and tools that are needed to integrate these structures into site-based professional learning (see Figure 1.4).

Part III features the concluding chapter (Chapter 9), which provides an opportunity for early education leaders to synthesize the content in Parts I and II and take the next steps toward directly applying learning at the site level. We discuss the role of the leader in establishing a culture of reflection and inquiry, and we support leaders in designing and rolling out a professional development system that is responsive to site-level needs. We recognize common pitfalls and discuss the problems encountered, and we offer resources for sustained capacity building.

Strategies, protocols, and additional resources are embedded throughout the book, providing practical tools for application in the field. At the conclusion of each chapter, we include a self-study section to support leaders in "taking the pulse" of their setting in order to determine appropriate and actionable next steps—at a single site or a network of sites.

PART I

Promoting Cornerstone Educator Competencies

CHAPTER 2

Using Executive Functions

Planning and Reflection in the Early Education Classroom

It's a chilly and slushy walk from the bus station to the Explorations Early Learning Center, but Maria brightens a bit when she thinks about the day ahead. Maria, a PreK teacher at the Center, has a special activity planned for the sensory table today and can hardly wait to see the looks on children's faces.

When center time begins, Maria joins the children who chose the sensory table. As planned, she brings some surprises with her: smocks, cups, a funnel, and a big bucket of snow. Maria exclaims, "We're going to do something different at the sensory table today!" pouring the snow into the table. The children shriek with delight, immediately digging into the icy powder.

As the children play, Maria tries to carry out her lesson plan. She begins explaining what "freezing" and "melting" are, but the children do not seem to understand—or at least do not seem to be paying much attention. As she tries to decide what to do to help the children focus on the information she is explaining, they begin throwing snow at each other. Maria quickly bursts out, "No throwing snow! If you don't stop, I'm going to close the table." This seems to work for the moment.

Maria is trying to stay calm, but before she has the chance to take her first deep breath, she hears arguing coming from the art table where children are making collages. She sees that they are quarreling over supplies, reminding her that she meant to search for extra glue sticks earlier. Maria calls over to Jada, her co-teacher, and asks if she knows where any glue sticks are, but Jada is busy in the bathroom where children are washing their hands. Maria yells over to the children at the art table to share, and then turns back to her group. She's trying to recall the science words she was teaching, but now can't remember them. As she struggles to bring these words to mind, several more children come over to the sensory table and push and shove one another to squeeze into a spot, eager to have a turn with the snow, too. With the added children at the table, the snow throwing commences once more. Maria recalls how excited she was about this activity this morning and realizes that now she just wants it to end.

Maria's experience is not a unique one. Her intent is to engage children and stimulate their learning, but there are several decision points and hot spots along the way that impede the cognitively stimulating, exciting experience she planned. To be sure, she is an experienced educator, and her creativity, enthusiasm, and ability to engage each child make her an invaluable teacher. Maria's goal of teaching children about the states of water, and her plan to explore snow in the sensory table in order to achieve this goal, is commendable. However, Maria made some decisions (and, in some cases, forgot to make some!) that affected her ability to achieve the goals of her lesson and consequently the quality of the learning experience for the children. She did not anticipate the challenge of teaching new content to children who were preoccupied, and therefore distracted, by such highly engaging materials, especially in the context of a surprise. And, while she thought ahead to gather materials like the cups and funnel for the sensory table, she did not similarly plan for the shortage of glue sticks at the art table. Likewise, she did not have plans in place for "predictable" challenges. She did not set expectations regarding how the snow could (and could not) be explored, and she did not proactively assure the children that each of them would have a turn at the sensory table. Maria thought she was prepared for the day, but as she sees everything falling apart, she wonders, "What went wrong?"

When we read about, or observe, teaching experiences like Maria's, it is relatively easy to think about what *should* have been done. Maria should have read a book about water and snow prior to the guided play activity, and she should have previewed the sensory table activity, including her expectations for behavior during it. Perhaps, she could have had a schedule posted so that the children would not have to worry about if or when they would get their turns with the snow, and one could imagine that a list of the science words she wanted to teach would have helped Maria keep them in mind. But if we have been there ourselves, we also know that setting goals for children's learning, designing lesson plans that address those goals, anticipating roadblocks, and then responding to unpredictable reactions in real time is, to put it mildly, challenging. Educators like Maria need to employ cognitive strategies, such as those associated with executive functions (EF), in order to best meet these challenging demands.

Here, we remind ourselves that the demand for and use of EF strategies is highly dependent on the context; what is happening around us either burdens or frees up these cognitive processes. We can see from Maria's experience that when classroom hot spots arise (i.e., children arguing over glue sticks, throwing snow, and pushing one another to gain access to a particular area) and a teacher's attention is needed in multiple parts of the room, it is difficult to carry out a plan, maintain focus, and use multiple skills at once to manage all of the competing demands. Likewise, when situations are escalating and the stakes become higher (i.e., children might get hurt), it is that much more difficult to come up with a plan or recall the strategies we have been taught for how to defuse a situation. In demanding moments like these, Maria still "has" her EF skills—they do not suddenly cease to exist—it's just that they are more difficult to deploy. There are indeed few professions where EF skills are as frequently taxed as in the field of early education.

In this chapter, we delve into EF skills and related strategies and discuss why the use of EF strategies is considered a cornerstone educator competency. We then describe ways in which we can support educators' consistent use of EF strategies. At the end of the chapter, we provide a tool for self-study that supports leaders in gauging the ways in which their own context supports this cornerstone competency.

What Goes into Executive Functions?

As illustrated in Figure 2.1, EF strategies involve cognitive processes and practices that feed intentional thoughts and actions (Zelazo & Carlson, 2012). These strategies help educators to generate plans, follow through on them, and even wisely change course when their original plans are not working. And, these cognitive processes are what support them to coordinate the use of several skills at once, focus on the task at hand, apply knowledge from past experiences to present situations, and build awareness of their own strengths and challenges (Diamond, 2006; Jones et al., 2013; Mezzacappa, 2004).

How does the early childhood educator deploy these EF strategies? Let's consider Maria. She is an experienced teacher, and we can imagine that if prompted, she could have foreseen some of the specific challenges that would likely occur during her sensory table activity. When educators anticipate challenges, and prepare for them ahead of time, they are using particularly enhanced EF strategies. Likewise, in the midst of this chaotic moment, enhanced EF strategies would have supported Maria to critically reflect as difficulties, such as lack of calmness and focus, arose, and then adjust her plan in

FIGURE 2.1. EF strategies for the early educator.

response. Utilizing EF strategies, she could have taken a step back and talked to the children about her expectations at the sensory table.

While we know that an individual's EF skills and strategies for using them develop most rapidly during the preschool years—and that we must nurture and scaffold the development of these strategies in young children—what gets much less attention is the growing evidence that the development of EF skills and strategies continues through adolescence and into adulthood (Zelazo & Carlson, 2012). In turn, our EF strategies benefit us throughout our lifetime. From running errands, to planning family gatherings, to multitasking as part of our professional lives, EF strategies are vital for engaging and maintaining our attention, self-control, flexibility, and awareness.

Why Are Executive Functions a Cornerstone Educator Competency?

As we mentioned earlier, there are arguably few professions in which the use of EF strategies is as crucial—and as frequently taxed—as early education. Why is this the case? Let's work through the interconnected factors featured in Figure 2.2. Young children's development of their own EF strategies hinges on learning environments where the educator consistently models and

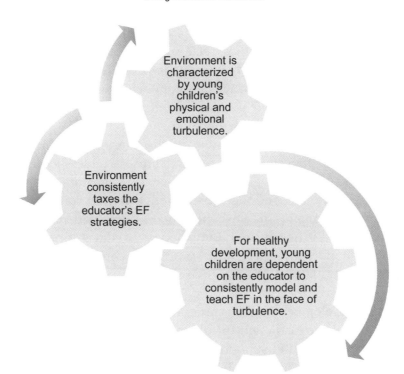

FIGURE 2.2. The early education paradox: Educators' enhanced use of EF strategies is consistently required *and* continually taxed.

teaches these skills (Institute of Medicine and National Research Council, 2015; McCoy, 2016). During the preschool years, children's EF skills, such as attention, response inhibition, and their ability to delay gratification, are still emerging; young children need lots of scaffolding in the domain of EF if they are to reach important developmental milestones. But here's the clincher: Because preschool-age children are in the midst of *developing* the very skills associated with their (lifelong) ability to regulate their own behavior, attention, and emotions, their classrooms are bound to be characterized by turbulence; challenging and unpredictable behaviors are part of the preschool child's daily life.

What does our understanding of children's developing EF skills mean for early educators? Well, recall how Maria's EF strategies were challenged when children began throwing snow at one another, arguing over glue sticks, and crowding the sensory table. During this (hardly extraordinary) classroom moment, children's abilities to inhibit responses and delay gratification were strained, creating a scenario in which Maria struggled to recall the vocabulary words she had planned to teach. Yes, she could have decided to teach the vocabulary terms during afternoon circle time instead, and then shifted her attention to deescalating the difficult situations in the various parts of the room. But in the midst of escalating classroom demands, accessing EF strategies to shift gears and generate a new plan, all the while remaining positive and constructive, is particularly challenging.

Leading young children in learning and discovery, while simultaneously striving to facilitate budding social relationships, is understandably taxing on educators' use of EF strategies. And when early educators' abilities to use EF strategies are strained, and then obstructed, there is a spiraling effect: As teachers struggle to maintain focus and remain calm, so do children—this, in turn, further taxes the educator. But when early educators are working in a context that supports their use of EF strategies—contexts in which leaders are cultivating regulated learning environments—even despite children's expected turbulence, they are able to draw on these strategies in order to fuel children's development and learning. In these contexts, the early educator engages in a cycle of thoughtful planning and subsequent implementation; she is encouraged and supported to think flexibly, problem solve, and adjust her instructional approach in real time in ways that are responsive to children. Through it all, in contexts that cultivate regulated learning environments, the early educator has tools that scaffold her process of reflection: She is constantly building awareness of her own strengths and challenges, as well as building her awareness of her own professional strengths and needs.

What Tools Do Early Educators Need to Support Their Use of Executive Functions in the Classroom?

We know that setting up and supporting early educators to use EF strategies at a high level is a crucial way for early education leaders to cultivate regulated and rigorous learning environments. After all, these are the skills and strategies educators draw on when designing instructional goals and plans, making instructional decisions in real time, and reflecting on these teaching experiences to develop professional knowledge and inform their future decisions. So, how can we support early educators to access and use their EF strategies to navigate the range of classroom situations? In our research and collaboration with early educators, we have developed and used several strategies that have become indispensable components of the early educator's toolbox of EF strategies and supports.

> ## Is There Something Else Going On?
> ### *Unintended Barriers to Using Enhanced EF Strategies*
>
> In this chapter, we discuss the tools that early educators need to support their use of EF strategies in the classroom, but we would be remiss if we did not take a moment to remind ourselves that tools can only go so far, and even those of us with the most enhanced EF strategies can't put them to use in the wrong circumstances. First and foremost, early learning settings must be characterized by stability and warmth and must genuinely promote open and respectful communication among adults. When these conditions are not met, educators are too stressed to respond to the expected "turbulence" of early childhood. It is therefore incumbent on leaders in the early education field to reflect on the ways in which working conditions can support educators to develop and leverage their strong EF strategies for positive, productive classroom interactions.

Here, we highlight tools focused on supporting *instructional planning* and *instructional reflection*. These EF-related competencies can be considered "power strategies" for the early educator—they are truly indispensable for strong teaching and productive learning. And although we are primarily focusing on planning and reflection, the ways in which we support educators to use these strategies simultaneously encourage and promote other EF strategies. For example, instructional planning necessarily involves *setting goals* that guide that plan, and likewise, strong reflection practices require *flexible thinking* on the part of the educator, such that various perspectives and possibilities are taken into account.

Tool 1: Instructional Planning

Instructional planning is already part of early educators' professional experience. This is true whether an early educator organizes her teaching around an

> Leaders can support early educator executive functioning by providing tools for:
>
> | Instructional Planning | Instructional Reflection |

emergent curriculum, a prescribed program, or something in between. No matter the curricular context, if the early educator is going to create strong learning opportunities for children, her daily responsibilities necessarily include thoughtful preparation to meet instructional goals. Here, we describe the characteristics of an instructional planning tool that optimally supports EF strategies—goal setting, planning, and flexible thinking.

"But We Already Have Planning Books . . ."

Early educators, like all educators, often have planning books or binders in which they record the instructional design of each day. When designed and used well, planning books and the various lesson forms and sheets, which are often provided and even required in early learning settings, have an important place. But in many cases, these planning tools and forms are not actually organized around supporting early educators' EF strategies. For example, some planning forms and books are designed to primarily ensure regulation compliance or to record learning objectives. While they have a place in guiding early educators' work, they often fail to focus on the thinking and procedures needed to create strong learning activities.

Here, we focus on how to design a planning tool that is, first and foremost, useful for instructional preparation and design. In your setting, think through the primary purpose of the planning tools available to you and whether and how these tools serve the intended purpose. You might tweak the tool according to the recommendations suggested here, you might design a new one, or you might find that what you have on hand is effectively getting the job done. The key is to ensure that educators' planning tools genuinely and strategically support just that—planning.

What Are the Characteristics of a Lesson Plan Tool That Supports Early Educators' Use of EF Strategies in the Classroom?

Here, we highlight four characteristics of a lesson plan tool that supports early educators' use of EF strategies in the classroom. At the end of the chapter, we provide a sample lesson planning tool you can use (see Figure 2.8).

Starts with the Goal. The lesson plan tool should begin with the end in mind. In other words, it should prompt early educators to, first and foremost, answer two questions: What skills and knowledge do I want children to gain from this learning experience? What learning activity will I use to accomplish these goals? The identified learning goal(s) and learning activity will act as touchstones for the rest of the planning process. Note that this goal and activity do not appear out of thin air, but are connected to a larger plan for classroom learning, such as a unit of study that revolves around a thought-provoking and engaging theme or topic. Figure 2.3 illustrates how Maria, in our case example, might complete the first step of the planning process. Notice that her learning goals include those focused on content knowledge and social skills.

Outlines the Four W's. Once the early educator has a learning goal and activity in mind, it is time to consider some of the plan's organization and logistics. In other words, the lesson plan tool should prompt the early educator to consider the four "W's":

- <u>Wh</u>o will participate (whole class or small group)?
- <u>Wh</u>ere will we do this activity?
- <u>Wh</u>en will we do this activity, and for how long?
- <u>Wh</u>at materials will teachers and children need?

Maria's plan was to conduct the learning activity with a small group of children at the sensory table during center time. Her materials included smocks, cups, a funnel, and a big bucket of snow. Using a planning tool to design this learning activity may have prompted her to consider the number of children and the amount of materials. For example, you can imagine that not having enough snow or cups for the children to use at the sensory table could lead to frustration, suddenly removing focus from learning and taxing the early educators' EF strategies in real time.

Lists Lesson Steps. In order to support early educators' EF strategies, the next aspect of the lesson planning process that this tool should capture is the progression of the learning experience—the steps that teachers and children will accomplish when moving through the learning activity. There is extensive guidance in the field about what goes into the design of an effective learning activity, most of which is based on the *gradual release of responsibility* model (Piaget, 1952; Vygotsky, 1978). This child-centered and developmentally sound instructional model begins with the teacher providing explicit instruction and modeling the learning goal in action and ends with the child assuming responsibility for the application of knowledge. One step-by-step approach to streamlining this model was recently coined by Nell Duke (2014, p. 100). Duke suggests the following lesson steps:

1. Tell me (i.e., introduce a lesson).
2. Show me (i.e., demonstrate the learning goal or activity, modeling steps and conveying content).

> **Learning Goal(s):** Children will (1) investigate snow while using descriptive language that demonstrates understanding of *freezing, melting, cold,* and *wet.* (2) practice turn taking.
>
> **Learning Activity:** Children will work together to explore snow and water at the sensory table.

FIGURE 2.3. Maria's plan.

3. Help me (i.e., support and guide children to engage in the learning activity).

4. Let me (i.e., allow children to apply the learning goal with increased independence, exploring freely while the teacher observes).

In Figure 2.4, we illustrate how Maria might have used this aspect of the planning tool.

Forecasts Pitfalls. The effective lesson plan tool will also support the early educator in putting her EF strategies to use by prompting her to mentally walk through the newly constructed plan with an eye toward potential pitfalls. That is, the tool should support the educator's flexible thinking by prompting her to anticipate (or "forecast") the kinds of common issues that often arise when young children are playing and learning together in a group or independently. By anticipating these potential snags in the plan, the early educator can then proactively devise strategies for dealing with them even before they happen, freeing her up in real time to spend her emotional and cognitive energy on the lesson and her students. This "instructional forecasting" part of the plan, for example, might ask early educators to consider children's prior knowledge (in terms of content and classroom procedures); assess the behavioral and social supports children might need to productively see the activity through; think about how to manage children's engagement and ability to focus when they are

---

Lesson Steps
(Tell Me, Show Me, Help Me, Let Me)

Before center time begins:
- **Tell** the children that they will explore snow at the sensory table. Explain how they will observe what snow feels and looks like, and that they will notice what happens as it changes temperature.
- **Show** the materials (smocks, cups, funnels, and snow) and model how to use them. Make sure to show children how to share funnels and model keeping the snow in the table. Use the words *melt, freeze, cold,* and *wet* as I model the activity.
- **Help** and guide the children to "act out" what they will do at the center. Think aloud as they follow expectations.
- **Remind** children that everyone will get a turn at the sensory table this week.

At the sensory table:
- **Review** the activity, learning goal, and how to use the materials.
- **Let** children explore the snow together. Ask them what they notice. Encourage them to use the words *melt, freeze, cold,* and *wet*.

FIGURE 2.4. Maria's step-by-step plan.

not actively participating in the activity (e.g., they are at a different learning center, or they are expected to sit quietly while a book is read); and plan what children should do if they finish early or require extra time. Figure 2.5 provides an example of a forecasting checklist that directs educators' attention to the task of anticipating pitfalls after they have created a lesson plan but before they have implemented it.

Think back again to Maria. If she were able to anticipate the excitement a new center activity might generate and predict the pushing and shoving that occurred as children vied for their turns, she might have been able to consider some preparatory steps that would have helped organize student participation. For example, simply having enough glue sticks at the art table could have made Maria's activity at the nearby sensory table go more smoothly.

Tool 2: Instructional Reflection

In the hustle and bustle of an early childhood learning setting, it sometimes feels as though the last thing early educators have time for is instructional reflection—they

> Leaders can support early educator executive functioning by providing tools for:
>
> | Instructional Planning | Instructional Reflection |

quickly must be thinking about the next goal, activity, and day! The fast-paced, always "on" nature of this profession does mean that the time and mental

---

☐ Do children need additional background knowledge to get the most out of this activity?

☐ Are there particular behavioral expectations that I should introduce or review?

☐ Are there materials that children will need to learn how to use or practice using?

☐ Are there times during the lesson when children are waiting or watching? How can I adjust the activity so that all children are actively engaged?

☐ If I am working with a small group, do children in other parts of the room know what they should be doing? How can I prepare them to be able to work and play without my immediate support?

☐ What should children do if they finish early? What should they do if they require more time?

FIGURE 2.5. Forecasting checklist.

---

space for in-depth reflection must be accommodated outside of the instructional setting—and the same is true for reflection about emotional responses, discussed in the next chapter. In our work with educators, in each and every professional learning community meeting (see Chapter 7) and coaching conference (see Chapter 8), educators have multiple opportunities for instructional reflection, such that it becomes part of the professional learning routine. Here we discuss the types of reflection prompts included in the reflection protocols that we have used to guide and support educators' EF strategies.

What Are the Characteristics of an Instructional Reflection Protocol That Support Early Educators' Use of EF Strategies in the Classroom?

An effective instructional reflection protocol does not have to be elaborate or complex—in fact, it shouldn't be! An effective protocol is simple and brief, with a limited number of reflective prompts that (1) orient the reflective conversation around the intended lesson plan, (2) encourage educators to consider both the strengths and challenges of the particular instructional event, and (3) steer plans going forward. Let's examine these aspects of instructional reflection in more detail and provide some examples. Figure 2.6 features a sample instructional reflection protocol that we have used to guide professional learning community meetings (see Chapter 7) and coaching conferences (see Chapter 8).

Orients the Reflective Conversation Around the Intended Lesson Plan. A first step in instructional reflection involves looking back at the intention. What was the goal of the lesson, activity, or transition? What were the steps children were meant to take? If a planning tool was used to prepare for the lesson, then this might be a good moment to formally look back at the plan as a quick refresher.

Examines What Went Well and What Was Challenging. Next, a reflection tool will prompt educators to think through the strengths and sticking points of the planned lesson, activity, or transition. When using a reflection tool to support educators in examining strengths and challenges, keep the following considerations in mind:

• Every instructional instance has *strengths*—even the worst moments become opportunities for growth. Likewise, the best teaching moments have room for tweaks or enhancements. It takes strong reflection skills to notice what is not immediately visible, and this is what needs to be worked on! For example, Maria, the PreK teacher, might have initially felt that the sensory

Date: _____

Lesson, activity, or transition I am reflecting on: _____

• What were my goals and expectations?

• What, specifically, went well?

• What, specifically, was challenging?

• How did I use my EF strategies?
  ○ Planning: What about my plan worked? What about my plan would I change?
  ○ Focus and follow-though: Did I use my plan to meet my goals?
  ○ Flexible thinking: How did I adjust my plan in the moment?

• What will I do next?

FIGURE 2.6. Example instructional reflection tool.

table activity was a mess, but she could have also noticed the specific ways in which the activity went well. For example, she piqued children's engagement, and the materials she gathered had the clear potential to support strong, inquiry-based learning. She could have revisited the plan and learning goals, working from that initial instance to recreate a successful lesson.

  • The more *specific* early educators' reflections are, the more useful they become for understanding and guiding future work. Sometimes, initial reflections are broad (e.g., "children were acting out" or "children enjoyed the activity"). This is a good first step. But then it is useful to examine exactly what transpired, as well as to identify specific antecedents to obstacles and specific mechanisms for engagement and learning. Maria, for example, could note several specific, related pitfalls, such as how children struggled to attend to her explanations while playing and did not know how to appropriately explore the snow. Then, once the specifics are enumerated, broader patterns might reveal themselves; in this case, the common thread appears to be that children needed to review and practice expectations *before* center time began.

• Instructional reflection is also a time when educators can think back on their use of EF strategies in particular, such as *planning* (i.e., preparing for learning activities); *self-control* (i.e., maintaining focus and follow-through); and *flexible thinking* (i.e., making adjustments and decisions in real time that are responsive to children's needs). In Maria's case, in the context of the sensory table lesson and activity, there were several factors that impeded her EF strategies in the moment. Prior to the lesson, she did not forecast, and prepare for, some of the difficulties that arose (e.g., children crowding the sensory table), and therefore, she was not prepared to address them; in turn, she lost focus (e.g., she couldn't remember the vocabulary terms she wanted to target) and struggled to problem solve. Remember, none of these points indicate that Maria lacks EF strategies! On the contrary, they are important data points that can help Maria understand the situations that overly tax her EF strategies.

Informs Future Plans. A reflection tool that supports educators' EF strategies connects instructional reflection to future planning in order to strengthen the link between self-awareness and improved practice. It is important to recognize that reflection and planning are tandem processes that support and enhance each other. In Chapter 9, we revisit the planning–reflection connection, focusing on cycles of inquiry for setting-level change. In Maria's case, she might use the insights gained from her reflections to tweak her process for instructional planning, such that she always incorporates "forecasting" pitfalls. She also might revise the way in which she introduces a new center— explaining, modeling, and practicing the activity *before* children begin and she puts the key materials in front of them.

Bringing It All Together: Leading Learning Settings That Promote Educator Executive Functions

When focused on enhancing early educators' EF strategies, we are reminded that the planning tools and protocols like those described here are *a platform for providing support*—they are not the support in and of themselves. For example, designing a lesson plan tool that focuses on EF strategies is an important first step, but it must be accompanied by ongoing guidance and structured collaboration. It is the responsibility of early education leaders to ensure that the planning and reflection tools provided are designed with intention (and educators' busy days in mind!). It is also their responsibility to reflect on how educators are supported in their use of these tools. For example:

- Are early educators provided with the time it takes to plan and reflect, beyond just completing forms?
- Are there structures in place for collaborative conversations that support this planning and reflection?
- Are there supports in place that help early educators use the time for planning, reflection, and collaboration in ways that make a difference for teaching and learning?

Use the self-study tool provided in Figure 2.7 to reflect on the ways in which early educators' effective EF strategies are supported in your context. We also provide a sample lesson plan tool for your use in Figure 2.8. Next, join us in Chapter 3, where we dig into the importance of attending to emotion regulation. We discuss how reflection not only supports high-quality instruction, but also self-awareness.

EF Strategies Early Educators Have and Use	What, exactly, is this strategy?	How do we support early educators' use of this strategy? (e.g., modeling its use daily, facilitating practice through professional development)	What else might we do to further support early educators' use of this strategy?
Planning	• Preparing learning activities that meet instructional goals are organized around steps that reflect how children learn, and include strategies for addressing anticipated challenges		
Reflecting	• Building awareness of instructional strengths and challenges and using these insights to guide future plans		

FIGURE 2.7. Self-study: Leading learning settings that promote educator EF.

Learning Goal(s):

Learning Activity:

The Four W's

Who will participate?

☐ whole group ☐ small group

Where will we do this activity?

When will we do this activity, and for how long?

What materials will teachers and children need?

Lesson Steps
(Tell Me, Show Me, Help Me, Let Me!)

FIGURE 2.8. Sample lesson plan tool.

CHAPTER 3

Effective Emotion Regulation

Managing Emotions for Improved Learning and Teaching

Jada, a second-year teacher, arrives at the Explorations Early Learning Center already tired. She was up late the night before with her toddler, trying to soothe him through his struggles with asthma. When Jada arrives, the room is already bustling with children—Maria, her co-teacher, was first to get there this morning. As Jada hangs up her coat, she recognizes an above-normal level of commotion in the room. Maria is trying her best to console two children who are already crying, and the sink in the corner seems to be clogged again and perhaps about to overflow. Jada notices that breakfast still needs to be put out—her first move should be to remedy that situation; however, she has one more thing to do to get ready to lead circle time.

Jada's body begins to feel tense, her heart starts to beat a little faster, and she realizes she is beginning to feel overwhelmed. "This is going to be a hard day," she thinks to herself, while also realizing only she can turn it around. As she tries to think of how to best relieve the mounting tension, she hears a loud crash. Jada turns to see that Anthony, a student who always seems to know how to push her buttons, has knocked down the castle Peter was working so hard to build. To make things worse, Anthony doesn't appear remorseful; Jada feels her resolve to stay calm and focused begin to dwindle. Thinking about her next steps to deescalate the situation, Jada approaches Anthony, just as he is swinging a block over his head, narrowly missing another child. "NO!" Jada yells, startling the children around her and causing one little girl to burst into tears.

Like her colleagues in early education and care settings across the country, Jada is working hard to carry out her professional mission to support young children's development. This entails undertaking the daily physical, emotional, and mental labor required of early childhood education—managing challenging behaviors and responding to unpredictable reactions—all while maintaining a focus on learning. In this particular moment, Jada strives to deploy her emotion regulation competencies. She tunes in to her own emotional response (i.e., feeling overwhelmed) and recognizes her need to use a coping strategy. These are two important—if not crucial—first steps. But in this case, her emotion regulation competencies are quickly taxed, and her ability to maintain a sense of calm and competence is diminished. As Jada perceives the situation to be worsening, her negative self-talk, which involves her thinking that it will be a hard day and perceiving Anthony as remorseless for breaking the castle, only exacerbates her difficult experience. To be sure, when Jada yells, "NO!" it is certainly not how early educators would want to respond to a challenging behavior presented in the classroom. However, Jada has not done irreparable damage and, at any moment, she can turn the situation around. One moment of rising tension does not have to yield "a hard day." In fact, relationship repairs after difficult interactions can actually be fruitful learning opportunities. Nevertheless, moments like these are stressful for all involved and thus should be kept to a minimum.

For early educators who have been through a morning like Jada's—the kind of experience in which stress mounts and it is hard to cope—it takes relatively little to be "pushed" over the edge toward an expression of emotion that doesn't help the situation. In this chapter, we discuss why this happens, and what goes into effective emotion regulation. We then describe strategies that early educators can use to contribute to their own emotion regulation and maintain a high-quality learning environment.

What Goes Into Effective Emotion Regulation for the Early Childhood Educator?

Emotion regulation involves being aware of one's own feelings, expressing them in ways that are appropriate for the situation, and managing a full range of feelings, including those that are negative (Denham, Bassett, & Zinsser, 2012). The constellation of competencies that go into emotion regulation helps us all maintain—or return to—a sense of calm, while persevering through challenging moments. While we all need these competencies, early educators must possess and use them to a very high degree (see Figure 3.1).

Effective emotion regulation for the early childhood educator means drawing on a variety of resources in the context of unpredictable and emotionally provocative situations (Jennings & Greenberg, 2009). As with EF strategies

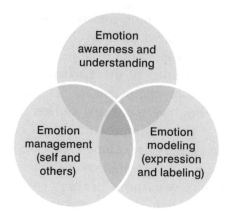

FIGURE 3.1. Emotion regulation skills for the early educator.

(see Chapter 2), early educators' abilities to deploy emotion regulation competencies depend on the situation. They must maintain emotion regulation in the face of escalating tension, and do so at a particularly high level if they are going to maintain their sense of calm and competence *and* support children in learning how to do the same.

Through modeling emotion regulation, early educators demonstrate for children, both explicitly and implicitly, how to respond to difficult situations. If handled appropriately, emotionally charged moments become teaching opportunities (Denham et al., 2012). Children consistently watch their teachers for cues, learning from the way they manage frustration, maintain control of the classroom, and respond to classmates who express anger, anxiety, or sadness at a particular time (Jennings & Greenberg, 2009; Jones et al., 2013). Modeling emotion expression not only involves communicating feelings in productive ways, but also concretely and consistently *labeling* emotions in real time—explicitly naming the feelings they experience, as well as those experienced by the children—to build children's emotion vocabulary and the classroom community's common language, norms, and routines.

What Does Effective Emotion Regulation Mean for Teaching and Learning?

When early educators are prepared to effectively regulate their emotions, and do so to a high degree, they are poised to cultivate high-quality learning environments. Jennings and Greenberg (2009) developed a research-based theoretical model to describe how emotion regulation, in tandem with the cultivation

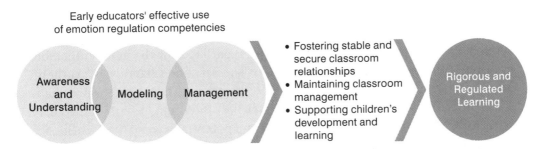

FIGURE 3.2. Early educators' effective emotion regulation contributes to high-quality classroom environments.

of strong relationships (see Chapter 4), contributes to a healthy classroom climate—and they focus on three concrete ways (see Figure 3.2) these cornerstone early educator competencies make a difference. Here, we briefly discuss how healthy classroom relationships, effective classroom management, and children's emotional development all depend on the teacher's effective emotion regulation.

Fosters Classroom Relationships

Adult–Child Relationships

We know that early educators' relationships with children are paramount to strong child development; in fact, early educators are considered attachment figures for young children (Howes & Spieker, 2016; Phillips, 2016). As with parent–child relationships, when these attachments are emotionally responsive, predictable, and secure, the benefits for children are tangible. A strong relationship between a child and her early educator is a mechanism for protecting her from the adverse effects of stress (Badanes, Dmitrieva, & Watamura, 2012) and promoting her engagement and sense of competence (Jones et al., 2013; Mashburn et al., 2008; Pianta, 2003; Raver, Garner, & Smith-Donald, 2007).

Peer–Peer Relationships

Early educators' emotion regulation also plays a role in the relationships children develop with one another. Early peer relationships are important for development, and when children are socially excluded or subordinated (i.e., they experience teasing, threatening behavior, or aggression) there are detrimental effects for early development, including social–emotional functioning and well-being (Obradović, Shaffer, & Masten, 2012; Phillips, 2016). In the classroom, early educators' emotional responses directly reflect how the children interact with one another, particularly with regard to how the more vulnerable children are treated. In Jada's case, when she responds harshly to Anthony after he destroys the castle, she models to the other children one way to handle a problem and treat a peer. Despite her best intentions to maintain safety within the classroom, Jada's reaction has the potential to negatively influence how children learn to treat each other. Conversely, taking a deep breath and calmly responding to Anthony's behavior, using clear language about the feelings associated with the situation, would positively model emotion regulation and also prevent a further escalation of negative emotion among the children in the classroom (i.e., the little girl would likely not burst into tears).

Maintains Classroom Management

Effectively managing a classroom requires early educators to maintain a sense of calm, feel themselves in control of the classroom, and use their own positive emotions to foster excitement for learning (Carlock, 2011; Jennings & Greenberg, 2009). For Jada, who is experiencing emotional distress, this means that, until she regains her cool, she will continue to experience difficulty in managing the classroom. Her negative behavior will influence the behavior of the children, which will then further challenge her own emotions.

Supports Children's Development and Learning

Children's Emotional Development

As we mentioned earlier, teachers have the potential to positively influence the development of children's emotion regulation in a number of ways. They can model strategies that enable them to effectively manage their own emotions and behaviors, engage children in warm and positive interactions, and explicitly teach children strategies that they can use to regulate their emotions (Carlock 2011; Jennings & Greenberg 2009; Jones et al., 2013; Maurer & Brackett 2004; Roeser et al., 2012). Even in Jada's case, where her emotion regulation skills were taxed to the point where she lost control, the moment still provides a learning opportunity—one in which Jada can demonstrate to the class how one might take steps to repair a situation gone wrong. These learning opportunities—through modeling and practice—are critical during this period of childhood when emotion regulation skills are developing rapidly and are in need of support.

Classroom Focus on Learning

When early educators' emotion regulation competencies are deployed in productive ways, not only do they support children's own emotion regulation development, they also create the conditions necessary for strong early learning opportunities. When early educators maintain a sense of calm and self-efficacy, they can then focus on teaching and learning. Recall that early educators' emotion regulation promotes effective classroom management. That is, classroom management has a reciprocal relationship with classroom learning opportunities: Children are more likely to stay on task and avoid problem behaviors when the environment is cognitively stimulating. In Jada's case, she has a rich plan for the day's learning activities, but under the circumstances, she would be hard-pressed to engage her students in deep learning unless she can regain control of her emotions.

What Strategies Do Early Educators Need to Support Their Emotion Regulation in the Classroom?

How can educators access their emotion regulation competencies in the classroom, even in the face of challenging situations? In our research and collaboration with early educators, we have developed and used several strategies that have become indispensable components of their emotion regulation toolbox. Here, we highlight strategies focused on:

Supporting Educators' Use of Emotion Regulation Strategies: Professional Development Is Key

Before we dive into emotion regulation strategies, however, it's important to keep in mind that supporting early educators' emotion regulation in the classroom does not mean "handing over" these strategies for independent use. Instead, supporting effective emotion regulation means that we must encourage, practice, and reinforce strategy use in the context of ongoing, collaborative learning communities (see Chapter 7), and then strengthen and refine educators' strategy use through classroom coaching for connected practice (see Chapter 8). In the context of these strong professional development structures, emotion regulation strategies are enhanced and particular strategies are made routine; in the absence of this meaningful support, uptake will be minimal, and educators' use of these strategies might miss the mark. With the importance of professional development in mind, we now turn to actual, doable strategies.

- supporting emotion awareness and understanding (i.e., observing and noticing, documenting, and reflecting); and
- promoting emotion management (i.e., addressing the physical signs of mounting negative stress and the thoughts and perceptions fueling that stress).

Over time, we can support early educators in using these emotion regulation strategies as a series of steps for maintaining—or returning to—a sense of calm and self-efficacy, even in difficult moments (see Figure 3.3).

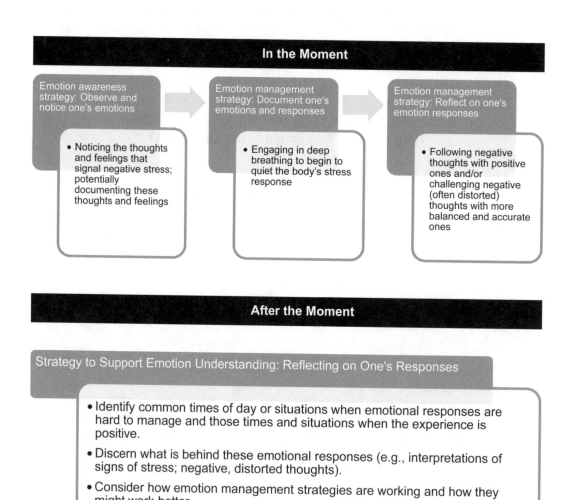

FIGURE 3.3. Steps for early educators' emotion regulation.

Strategies to Develop Emotion Awareness and Understanding: Observation, Documentation, and Reflection

Observation, documentation, and reflection are already part and parcel of quality early education practices. However, these strategies are typically focused on cultivating early educators' awareness of the strengths and needs of the children in their classroom. Here,

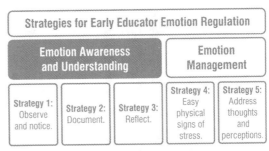

Strategies for Early Educator Emotion Regulation	
Emotion Awareness and Understanding	**Emotion Management**

Strategy 1: Observe and notice.	Strategy 2: Document.	Strategy 3: Reflect.	Strategy 4: Easy physical signs of stress.	Strategy 5: Address thoughts and perceptions.

we take a different approach—one focused on the early educators' emotional responses to daily classroom situations (i.e., feelings in the body or mind, automatic thoughts, knee-jerk reactions), as well as the interactions that precede and follow these responses. What might assessing early educators' emotion awareness look like in the classroom? We separate emotion awareness and understanding into a few key parts.

Strategy 1: Observe and Notice One's Emotions

When early educators take their "emotional pulse," they are responding mindfully and intentionally to the situation at hand. But let's be clear: In the midst of an emotionally provocative and fast-moving situation, stepping back to consider one's response is not easy. It's an abstract and cognitively sophisticated act that proves challenging even in relatively calm circumstances. In our collaboration with educators, we have found that a co-constructed, concrete, visual tool that frames the way we tune in to emotional responses can facilitate educators' use of this emotion regulation technique. We created a scale from 1 to 5 to map responses to classroom moments and dubbed it our "Stress-O-Meter" (see Figure 3.4 for a filled-in example and Figure 3.5 for a blank version for your use). It is worth mentioning that a certain amount of "stress" is healthy and necessary for early educators to feel motivated and to do their job well. With a healthy level of stress (a level 3 on the Stress-O-Meter), educators can feel both focused and energized. However, the two extremes on the scale are not healthy: a hard-to-manage amount of stress that is accompanied by a loss of energy or a hard-to-manage amount of stress that is accompanied by intense or frantic energy. Both affect one's motivation and efficacy. In these situations, it is much more difficult for educators to access and use what they know about good teaching, and their stress response can inhibit them from doing their best work. We encourage teachers to pause throughout the day and

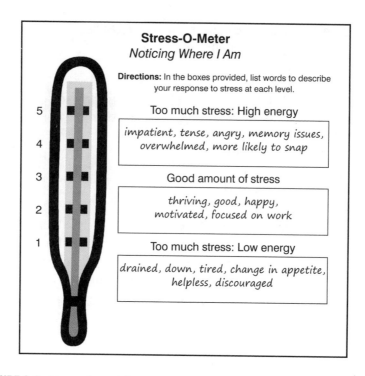

FIGURE 3.4. Example tool for noticing emotion responses: Stress-O-Meter.

notice where their stress level falls on the Stress-O-Meter. It might be helpful to post the Stress-O-Meter in a place that is easily accessible in order to prompt these observations.

Additionally, it is worth emphasizing that the language descriptions featured in the Stress-O-Meter are generated by the teachers with whom we collaborated. We have found that educators' input about the language and features of this tool have been crucial in successfully supporting their emotion regulation.

Strategy 2: Document One's Emotions and Responses

Once educators have a shared tool (and a shared language) for noticing their responses to everyday classroom situations—like the Stress-O-Meter featured in the previous section—we can then support educators to document these responses. Why bother documenting? Well, when early educators *consistently* and *formally* document their responses, and the factors triggering these responses, they are collecting very important data. Over time, patterns in classroom emotions emerge, and trends in reactions and interactions take shape. Also, sometimes the simple act of writing something down can help us gain perspective in the moment (Pennebaker & Smyth, 2016).

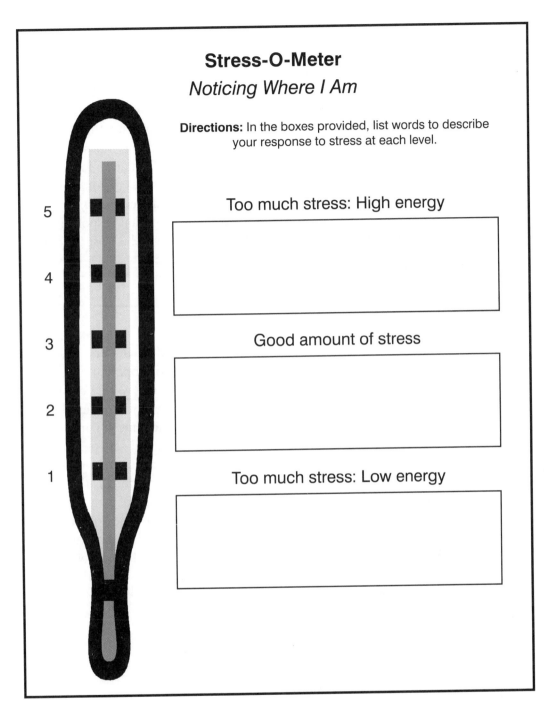

FIGURE 3.5. Tool for noticing emotion responses: Stress-O-Meter.

In our collaboration with educators in designing an effective tool for documenting responses, our partners let us know that this tool should feature a space to briefly document what was noticed. In other words, documentation should not be a time-consuming process. Ultimately, we found that jotting down a minimal amount of information on a Post-it Note a few times a week, often using shorthand, was feasible and garnered useful information for reflection. We called these "stress log Post-it Notes" (see Figure 3.6). For some teachers, the shorthand incorporated the Stress-O-Meter's scale: educators would write the number, from 1 to 5, that represented their emotional response and a quick note about what adults and children were doing. The Post-it Notes shown in Figure 3.6 are samples from participating teachers.

Strategy 3: Reflect on One's Emotion Responses

When educators reflect on what they have noticed and documented, their emotion awareness begins to grow into emotion understanding. But the teacher who is working hard to support children's learning and development does not always have the time or mental space for in-depth reflection. While the fast-paced nature of early childhood teaching should not prevent teachers from reflecting on emotional responses, keep in mind that the time for in-depth reflection must be accommodated outside of the instructional setting. In our work with educators, in each and every professional learning community meeting (see Chapter 7) and coaching conference (see Chapter 8), the educators have multiple opportunities to reflect on their corpus of documented "noticings." They support one another to identify common times of the day or situations when hot spots arise, as well as those times of day and practices that promote their best teaching and children's best learning. These facilitated reflections centered on building emotion understanding take several forms, depending on the context and goal.

FIGURE 3.6. Example tool for documenting emotional responses: Stress-log Post-it Notes.

Reflective Prompts. Sometimes, educators can rely on open-ended questions such as "What do you notice?"; "What made this challenging?"; "What went well?"; "What patterns do you observe?" At other times, they can use more specific, though open-ended, prompts to zero in on a particular emotion regulation goal: "What times of day are consistently challenging?"; "What tends to happen when you react in a particular way?"; "What thoughts go through your mind during challenging moments?"

Sorts and Charts. Early educators can also employ this reflection task to sort situations or responses into categories, as well as to chart aspects of what they noticed in order to identify patterns. For example, educators might pool their collective challenging moments and sort them by those situations that are in their control and those that are out of their control (we have noted that we often find that situations end up somewhere in between). Alternatively, educators might, together, complete a chart that organizes challenging situations by time of day, setting, children's behavior, and/or adults' behavior. It is always helpful to look for patterns and to isolate areas for targeted support.

Graphic Organizers. Sometimes, cultivating emotion regulation competencies requires a more structured reflection procedure. In these cases, early educators can turn to a graphic organizer (i.e., a visual "map" that uses symbols to express the relationships between ideas, thoughts, or events). For example, when reflecting on the ways in which one's own emotion responses influence children's responses, educators can check the responses on the graphic organizer, titled "Stress Flows," featured in Figure 3.7.

Emotion Management Strategies: Addressing Physical Signs of Mounting Negative Stress Along with Thoughts and Perceptions Fueling That Stress

When we support educators' emotion awareness and understanding by practicing and encouraging observation, documentation, and reflection, we are taking an important step toward creating the conditions in which educators can use and enhance their emotion regulation competencies. Another important step is to support educators' emotion management strategies. The key value of emotion awareness is being

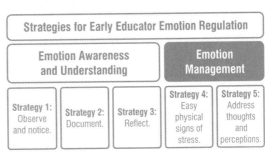

Strategies for Early Educator Emotion Regulation

Emotion Awareness and Understanding			Emotion Management	
Strategy 1: Observe and notice.	Strategy 2: Document.	Strategy 3: Reflect.	Strategy 4: Easy physical signs of stress.	Strategy 5: Address thoughts and perceptions.

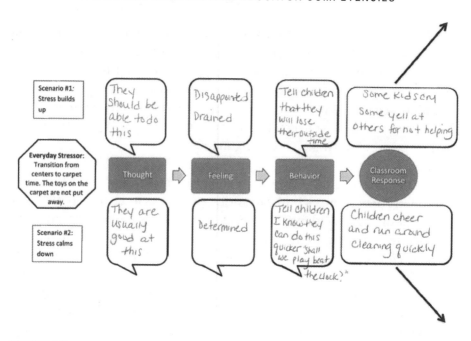

FIGURE 3.7. Example graphic organizer to support emotion reflection: Stress flows.

able to use this heightened understanding to steer responses, and for educators, this entails using effective emotion management strategies. What are effective emotion management strategies for the classroom? Here, we focus on two types: easing the physical signs of stress and addressing the thoughts and perceptions that fuel stress.

Strategy 4: Ease the Physical Signs of Stress in the Classroom

When emotions intensify, they are experienced in the mind and the body. Jada's experience highlights this: her body is tense, her heart is racing, and she feels overwhelmed. For early educators more generally, once they identify these responses, the next step is to ease the physical signs of stress in order to calm the mind and think clearly. While seemingly simplistic, slow and conscious breathing actually counters the body's automatic stress response and reduces the signs of stress. In our collaboration with educators, we drew on the extensive research that points to conscious, deep breathing as a powerful technique for regaining emotional equilibrium (Porges, Doussard-Roosevelt, & Maiti, 1994). Breathing slowly and deeply does not have to take long, and more important, it does not require educators to step away from the situation the way other relaxation strategies might entail.

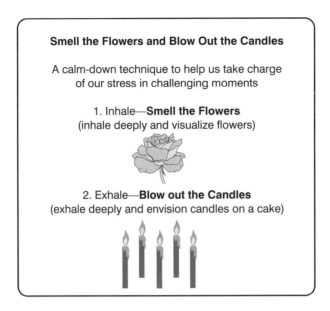

FIGURE 3.8. Classroom poster: Smell the flowers and blow out the candles.

Additionally, when early educators use deep breathing, they are not only helping to restore their own emotional equilibrium, but are also modeling for children how they can use the same technique themselves. Therefore, we offer educators tools that focus on teaching both educators and children deep-breathing strategies to regain calm and focus. This tool might take the form of telling children to "Smell the flowers and blow out the candles." Figure 3.8 represents a visual aid that teachers can post in their classrooms as a reminder to children (and themselves!) to use the deep-breathing strategy when faced with a challenging moment. In this simple and engaging breathing technique, children learn to visualize a bunch of flowers to smell—that's the inhale—and birthday candles to blow out—that's the exhale. (If you add pictures of flowers and birthday candles, you can make a larger-size deep-breathing poster to use in your classroom.)

Strategy 5: Address Thoughts and Perceptions in the Classroom

If educators are engaging in the emotion regulation strategies described thus far, they have consciously observed the thoughts and feelings that signal mounting negative stress, potentially jotting these thoughts and feelings down. Then, they have engaged in deep breathing to begin to quiet their physical stress response.

Ideally, these steps toward positive and productive emotion regulation happen swiftly and in the moment. Then, with their composure and calm restored, educators are poised to take the next step in emotion management: addressing the thoughts (or "cognitions") that are potentially fueling their difficult experiences. We recommend that educators use two specific cognitive strategies, commonly found in the psychology literature, to target the thoughts that fuel stress.

Follow Negative Thoughts with Positive Ones. In difficult situations, the mind, often subconsciously, engages in a continuous stream of "self-talk" that can become increasingly negative. For early educators, these negative thoughts compound, rather than alleviate, a challenging classroom experience. However, by purposefully following what might be an automatic negative thought with a positive one, educators can steer their minds toward more constructive and beneficial thinking. For example, in Jada's instance, she might follow her negative thought, "This is going to be hard day," with a more positive thought, such as, "I've handled difficult mornings before, and I will be able to handle this one." In our work with teachers, we supported them in generating their own, individualized positive thoughts on which they could rely during difficult classroom situations. Specifically, we encouraged them to identify a visual image—a person, place, or object—that brought them a sense of calm. Then, we asked them to generate a positive phrase or sentence that resonated with them. Teachers then committed to bringing this paired image and phrase to mind when they experienced negativity in order to bring positive thoughts to the forefront.

Challenge Negative Thoughts. A second strategy for addressing negative thoughts is to directly challenge them. For many educators, the negative thoughts that might flood their minds during a troubling situation are usually inaccurate (i.e., "I'm a terrible teacher!") or distorted (i.e., "These children never clean up!"). What's more, when their thinking is clouded by high levels of stress, and therefore becomes inaccurate and distorted, educators' negative feelings are reinforced and their ability to draw on their emotion regulation competencies diminished. What does challenging negative thinking in the classroom look like? In our work with teachers, we presented them with the most common thought distortions identified in the psychology literature (see Table 3.1). Teachers then identified the distortions that seemed most familiar and discussed their experiences with these kinds of negative thoughts. Next, we practiced challenging negative thoughts, using brief classroom cases as a platform for practice, both in the moment and during reflection conversations. For example, a teacher who remembered thinking, "I'm not very good

TABLE 3.1. Common Categories of Thought Distortions

Cognitive distortion	What is it?	Classroom examples
Mind reading	You assume you know what people are thinking.	"That parent doesn't care about her child."
Fortune-telling	You predict the future, thinking things will get worse.	"My co-teacher is out, so this is going to be a terrible week."
Catastrophizing	You believe events to be so awful, you can't handle them.	"It will be a disaster if I don't get this portfolio done."
Personalizing	You blame yourself for negative events.	"The children are misbehaving because I am a bad teacher."
Overgeneralizing	You come to an overall conclusion about a person or situation based on a single event.	"These children never clean up."
All-or-nothing thinking	You view people, events, or situations as all good or all bad.	"All of the planning that went into that activity was a waste of time."
"Shoulds"	You interpret events based on how you think things *should* be, rather than focusing on how they actually are.	"He should be able to write his name by now."
Emotional reasoning	You let your feelings guide your interpretation of reality.	"I feel useless, so I know I'm a bad teacher."

Note. Adapted from Leahy (2003).

at teaching," then weighed the evidence that made the thought true (i.e., "I didn't stop a conflict today and one child hurt another") and the evidence that made the thought false (i.e., "I've helped lots of children learn how to make safe choices, write their names, and enjoy books"), was able to create a more balanced and accurate thought (i.e., "I'm still figuring out how to help this child learn how to calm down before he lashes out, but that doesn't mean I'm a terrible teacher—I'm a good teacher who's trying her best to support her students' learning and safety"). We also used a handout (see Figure 3.9) in order to support educators as they countered their negative thoughts.

Why focus on what teachers are *thinking*? The reason is that thoughts, emotions, and behaviors are tightly linked. An overly negative thought can directly fuel unmanageable feelings of stress, and, in turn, unproductive reactions to the situation at hand. Circling back to Jada, as she perceives the classroom

Challenge Negative Thoughts

You can use these three steps to challenge your negative thoughts. Here is an example from an early childhood teacher.

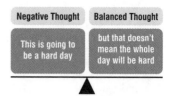

Steps to Challenging Negative Thoughts	Example
Step 1: Identify your negative thought.	• This is going to be a hard day.
Step 2: Think of the evidence you have that makes the thought true.	• Lots of children are making a mess. • A few children are crying.
Step 2: Think of evidence you have that makes the thought false.	• I can't see into the future—I don't actually know what this day will be like. • I often have a difficult morning and then things get better.
Step 3: Create a more balanced thought.	• The morning was hard, but that doesn't mean the whole day will be hard. I can handle this and get the children ready for our activity.

Now, try these steps using one of your own negative thoughts.

Steps to Challenging Negative Thoughts	My Thinking
Step 1: Identify your negative thought.	
Step 2: Think of the evidence you have that makes the thought true.	
Step 2: Think of evidence you have that makes the thought false.	
Step 3: Create a more balanced thought.	

FIGURE 3.9. Handout: Challenge negative thoughts.

situation to be worsening, her thoughts contribute to her experiences of difficulty, and she reacts impulsively, yelling at her students and exacerbating the moment of high stress. The two strategies we described are useful in such a moment in order to frame and guide reflection conversations during professional learning community meetings or coaching conferences.

Bringing It All Together: Leading Regulated Early Learning Settings

To maintain a steady sense of calm and to draw on energy that is motivating, early educators can and must call upon a wealth of regulatory resources: tuning in to their emotional responses, understanding what underlies these responses, and then using emotion management strategies to ease difficult emotions when they do (inevitably!) arise. When early educators are given the support they need to effectively regulate their emotions, and do so to a high degree, they are poised to cultivate high-quality learning environments where relationships flourish, transitions and routines run smoothly, and children's learning and development are continuously promoted.

What does this all mean for early education leaders? It means that if we do not attend to the ways in which the working conditions and professional supports that we put in place enable (or hinder) early educators' emotion regulation, then we cannot expect them to consistently and expertly deploy enhanced emotion regulation strategies. It is up to all leaders, whether early education supervisors and directors or district and state decision makers, to cultivate regulated learning environments where early educators can do their best work. To do so, educators need to experience ongoing professional development that targets the strategies described in this chapter—strategies that support early educators to access and use their emotion regulation competencies in the classroom.

Use the self-study tool provided in Figure 3.10 to reflect on the ways in which early educators' effective emotion regulation is supported in your learning context. Next, join us in Chapter 4, where we explore the importance of attending to a close companion of emotion regulation: relationship building.

Emotion Regulation Strategies Early Educators Have and Use	What, exactly, is this strategy?	How do we support early educators' use of this strategy? (e.g., modeling its use daily, facilitating practice through professional development)	What else might we do to further support early educators' use of this strategy?
Emotion awareness strategy: Observing one's emotional responses in the classroom	• Noticing the thoughts and feelings that signal the educator's own negative stress; potentially documenting these thoughts and feelings		
Emotion understanding strategy: Reflecting on one's emotional responses	• Identifying common times of day or situations when emotional responses are challenging or positive • Discerning what underlies these emotional responses		
Emotion management strategy: Easing physical signs of mounting negative stress	• Engaging in deep breathing to begin to quiet the body's stress response		
Emotion management strategy: Addressing thoughts and perceptions fueling stress	• Following negative thoughts with positive ones and/or challenging negative (often distorted) thoughts with more balanced and accurate ones		
Emotion understanding strategy: Reflecting on one's use of emotion management strategies	• Considering how emotion management strategies are working and how they might work better		

FIGURE 3.10. Self-study: Reflecting on effective talk for emotion regulation strategies.

CHAPTER 4

Cultivating Strong Relationships
Developing Children's Relational Skills
by Starting with Educators

Jada approaches the PreK room at the Explorations Early Learning Center with a smile on her face. She had missed the children when she was out part of last week caring for her son, and is happy to be back this Monday morning. But Jada's smile fades quickly as she steps into her classroom and takes in the glue-covered hands, shoes, floors, and tables. In one area, Maria and a group of children are doing papier-mâché; the rest of the classroom, through Jada's eyes, is filled with overstimulated children—children running around and using "outside" voices, as they track the paste on their shoes around the room.

"Boys and girls—what are we doing?" Jada asks, with an edge to her voice. Maria smiles and excitedly responds for the children, "We're making papier-mâché planets!" Jada glances at the lesson plan posted on the wall and confirms there is no mention of papier-mâché today. "I didn't know we were doing a hands-on project this morning," Jada replies, brow lifted and jaw slightly clenched. Maria continues stirring glue and water as she explains, "I decided that the kids would really love to do a special one today." She hesitates and then continues, "You were out again on Friday, so I couldn't check with you."

Jada turns around before rolling her eyes or saying something she would regret. She puts her things down and grabs a paper towel to begin cleaning the paste-covered floor tiles. Her thoughts begin on an all-too-familiar train: "Maria should have stuck to the original plan that I put a lot of work into. Besides, it's not my fault my son was sick. Maria knows I can't take him to child care when his asthma flares up."

Jada sighs loudly and calls the first few children, Danya, Marco, and Jordan, over to the sink so she can clean their shoes. Wiping vigorously and nodding her head from side to side, Jada huffs, "We have a big mess to clean up, breakfast isn't even out yet, and it's almost 9:30." She can't help but feel like she does everything.

Maria is busy at the art table, but hears Jada's comment and notes her prickly tone. "Why is she so mad?" Maria wonders to herself. "Jada says she wants more hands-on art. And it always seems like she wants me to do more of the lesson planning. Now I make a plan—with hands-on art!—and she's mad?"

Meanwhile, Jada turns from Danya's sneakers to Marco's. Marco senses Jada's anger and wonders if he did something wrong. His lower lip begins to tremble. Jada grabs Marcos's foot a little tighter as she scrubs and says, "Why are you crying? I'm the one who has to clean up this mess."

Jada and Maria are in the midst of a common struggle—one between two coworkers collaborating in close quarters in the emotionally charged and unpredictable context that is the early education classroom. Everyone has experienced something similar, whether in a co-teaching situation or through another instance of professional collaboration. Understanding the same experience from two conflicting perspectives is challenging. Disagreements are unavoidable, but communicating along the way, especially as hot spots arise and decisions are made, can help prevent these disputes and/or resolve them constructively when they do arise.

Having a comfortable distance from Jada and Maria's classroom, perhaps it is evident how seeking to understand another's perspective, while sharing one's own, could have helped in this moment. However, amid the clamor that often typifies the early childhood classroom, deploying these relational skills can be particularly difficult. Nonetheless it is imperative that, in an environment where children glean so much from adult modeling, educators have and use strong relational skills (National Scientific Council on the Developing Child, 2004).

In this chapter, we analyze the skills required to cultivate strong relationships, and discuss why this set of skills is paramount in the early childhood classroom. We then identify strategies for supporting educators. We conclude with tools that support building and maintaining stronger systems of professional relationships.

What Goes into Cultivating Strong Relationships?

The capacity to effectively cultivate strong relationships is central to satisfaction and success in everyday experiences, whether in the workplace, community, or as part of family life. At the core of this capacity is a set of competencies that supports positive interactions with others. By "positive interactions" we do not mean "the absence of conflict," but we do mean that everyday disagreements or tensions—inevitable in any collaboration—are met with constructive communication. Specifically, as illustrated in Figure 4.1, cultivating strong relationships requires:

- perspective taking and empathizing (i.e., seeing others' points of view as valid and viewing them with understanding, even when they are different from our own);
- understanding and interpreting social cues, such as language, facial expressions, and tone of voice, as well as others' behaviors, which allow us to decipher the perceptions and feelings that underlie the actions and words of others;
- navigating social situations, including those that are conflictual (i.e., engaging in open and respectful dialogue that seeks to understand the other's point of view and making reasonable concessions while considering one's own needs); and
- working in collaboration with others through mutual understanding and cooperation (Jones & Bouffard, 2012; Jones et al., 2013).

In the early childhood classroom, it is imperative that perspective taking is responsive to children's developmental stages and situational needs. For

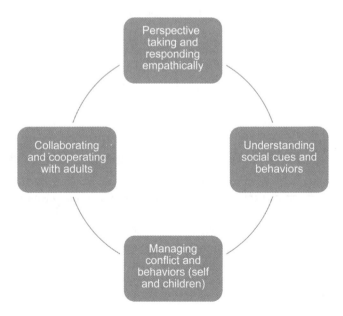

FIGURE 4.1. Relational competencies for the early learning classroom.

Jada and Maria, this would involves understanding, or seeking to understand, Marco's perception of his teachers' interaction over the art project and the resulting mess. The child senses tension in the room, internalizes it, and falls back on his relational and communication strategy in a time of stress: crying. In this case, Marco is swept into the cascade of conflict; Jada's relational skills are too taxed for her to effectively deploy empathy or soothe her student, and she is therefore unable support him in this moment.

In this way, relational skills in the classroom also involve taking preventive and responsive steps to manage children's social actions and behaviors. While early educators are negotiating their own classroom interactions, they are also engaging in behaviors and strategies that scaffold children's prosocial development and actions. This positive behavior management entails, for example, setting appropriate limits for children using a calm, firm tone in the face of their escalating emotions.

In addition, as demonstrated by Jada and Maria, the ability to collaborate with adults, particularly co-teachers, is an often overlooked, but *hugely important,* aspect of relational competence in the classroom. In the majority of early childhood classrooms, educators operate as a team, and the efficacy of this collaboration rests on their ability to plan, negotiate decisions, and problem solve together in the moment and over time.

Why Are Strong Relational Skills a Cornerstone Educator Competency?

Preschoolers are in the process of developing the skills associated with their lifelong ability to regulate their own behavior, attention, and emotions, a process that is correlated with their academic and personal success. Therefore,

Where Do Leaders' Relational Skills Fit In?

When considering the ways in which the educator's relational skills affect all of the relational skills in the classroom, it is important to remind ourselves that for Jada, Maria, and their colleagues across the nation, their day-to-day interactions and working relationship depend on the system of relationships in and around the setting itself (Jennings & Greenberg, 2009). Interpersonal interactions in a school or center are all a part of an interconnected system (Figure 4.2). In this sense, none of us are off the hook when it comes to mindfully cultivating and working hard at strong relationships—and we know it's some of the hardest work out there—for the benefit of children's learning and development.

even in the midst of a challenging work environment, educators must possess and deploy enhanced relational competencies to promote early learning and development. After all, relationships are the proverbial soil in which children's social–emotional skills grow (Jones & Bouffard, 2012)—and these same relationships fuel the development of children's language, literacy, and other academic skills.

When educators cultivate enhanced relational skills, and are supported by leaders to use them, how does this particular set of competencies form the "soil" for children's learning? We focus next on three key ways that educators' deployment of relational skills contributes to a healthy classroom environment.

Relational Skills Affect the Quality of Classroom Relationships

Not surprisingly, early educators' relational skills influence *all* relationships in the early education and care setting—those between the educator and her students, between co-teachers, between teachers and parents, as well as those among the site's staff, and, most important, the children in their care (see Figure 4.2). In fact, when educators struggle to deploy constructive relational skills, especially during tense moments, learning opportunities are missed both because conflict takes up time and because the experience of stress reduces educators' abilities to teach and children's capacities to learn (Phillips, 2016). On the other hand, when these systems of relationships are stable and secure, they protect children from the adverse effects of stress (Badanes, Dmitrieva, & Watamura, 2012) and promote their engagement with and feelings of competence about school (Jones et al., 2013; Mashburn et al., 2008; Pianta, 2003; Raver et al., 2007).

Relational Skills Affect Classroom Management

Effective classroom management requires that the educator set up routine interactions and systems that encourage children's collaboration and conflict management, consistently and calmly assert appropriate limits and guidance, and support preventive and responsive steps to manage children's social actions and behaviors (Jennings & Greenberg, 2009). Recalling the vignette that opened this chapter, we can see how Jada and Maria's challenges in negotiating a potential conflict contributed to a downward spiral in classroom management. In this instance, they were not on the same page regarding the morning's activity, and their strained exchange and tense demeanors contributed to their difficulties in keeping children's behavior and the relational environment constructive and positive.

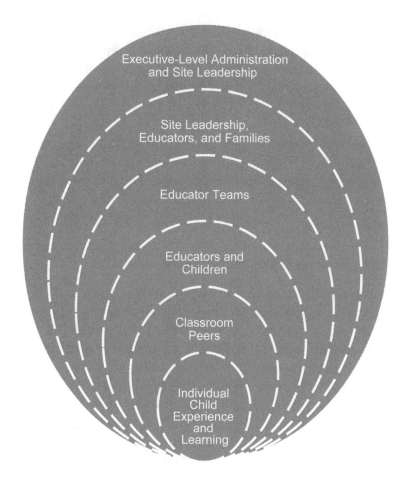

FIGURE 4.2. Systems of relationships that influence children's experiences and learning.

Early Educators' Relational Skills Affect
Children's Relational Skills

Under optimal conditions, teachers have a very strong, positive influence on the development of children's relational skills. This influence is manifested in a number of ways: by modeling strategies that enable children to effectively manage their behaviors and respond appropriately to the behaviors of others, by engaging children in warm and positive interactions, and by explicitly teaching children strategies they can use to build and sustain relationships (Carlock, 2011; Jennings & Greenberg 2009; Jones et al., 2013; Maurer & Brackett, 2004; Roeser et al., 2012). It is a relationally attuned (or "in-tune") educator who can best tailor her instructional responses and communicative approach to the individual child's developmental, situational, and learning needs.

How Can We Support Early Educators' Relational Skills in the Classroom?

In our field collaborations with early educators, we have found that creating the conditions for early educators to deploy their relational skills, and supporting them to do so, involves strategies that are interpersonal themselves. These strategies leverage regular meetings, whether they are formally set up as professional learning community (PLC) meetings or regular staff meetings, as testing grounds for relational skills, such that educators discuss and grapple with this set of competencies in a safe and supportive context. Here, we highlight strategies focused on:

- co-developing, modeling, and reflecting on group norms that represent relational skills; and
- using resonant, brief case examples as a platform for applying relational skills.

Strategy 1: Co-Develop, Model, and Reflect on Group Norms That Represent Relational Skills

One strategy for leveraging meetings among educators toward enhanced relational skills is co-developing, modeling, and reflecting on group norms—or relational "ground rules"—that promote open dialogue, participation, trust, and productive work (Richardson, 1999). These norms act as guideposts for interactions and serve as a group commitment to agreed-upon ways of interacting and communicating. In what follows, we walk through how to establish group norms and put them to good use.

Co-Develop Norms

Why co-develop norms as part of regular meetings, such as PLCs and staff meetings? Well, this practice heightens group members' awareness of the relational skills required for productive professional conversations. What's more, by co-developing the norms, members feel an increased ownership over the expectations set, and therefore can commit to them and put them to use more authentically and consistently.

When brainstorming and consolidating the group's list of norms, it is important to ensure that these norms represent core relational skills. While some norms might be more procedural (i.e., timing), most should serve to establish the group's commitment to perspective taking, collaboration, and problem solving. With this in mind, when co-developing norms, it can be helpful to have categories of norms, including those focused on relational skills, available to guide the group brainstorm. In our work, we adapted categories presented by Richardson (1999), starting with one that connects procedures to respect for others.

- *Time*—when we meet and expectations for starting and ending on time (i.e., we commit to arrive on time and end on time).
- *Participation*—how and when we talk and listen (i.e., we will share talk time).
- *Confidentiality*—what we do, and don't do with regard to sharing outside of PLCs or other meetings (i.e., we will not discuss what we learn about students outside of meetings).
- *Approach with others*—how we manage conversations and regard one another (i.e., we will remember that everyone is well-meaning, and we will respect others' points of view).

Using these categories as guideposts, PLC members, or members of any community that meet regularly, can then develop norms that capture relational skills in ways that resonate with them. Figure 4.3 presents a list of norms established in one of our PLCs.

Model Norms

Of course, developing and posting relation-focused norms in a visible, meaningful place is just a start. To be effective, norms need to be posted and consistently modeled and applied. Whether educators are participants or facilitators during meetings, they have ample opportunities to model relational skills in

We will . . .

- keep confidential what we talk about in our meetings.
- be open to a different point of view.
- respect each other's opinions.
- agree to disagree when necessary.
- make our best efforts to come to our meeting on time.
- listen patiently, giving colleagues time to share their thoughts.
- listen respectfully and actively (no side conversations).
- try our best to understand each other's ideas.

FIGURE 4.3. Sample group norms.

Protocols to Guide Meetings

The National School Reform Faculty (NSRF) Harmony Education Center offers 200+ protocols and activities for professional learning, including a protocol for "Forming Ground Rules," developed by Marylyn Wentworth, that provide steps for co-developing group norms. Check out this resource, and other professional learning resources, at *www.nsrfharmony.org.*

real time. For example, they can take the time to explicitly consider the perspectives of other group members, highlighting the likely perspectives of the children and parents discussed in problem-solving conversations. They can also listen attentively and actively as group members, and share and respond empathically (nonverbally or verbally) when professional difficulties are described.

Reflect on Process

Using norms as an anchor when reflecting on group processes also directs the conversation to the concrete relational skills to which the group is committed. This reflection may be a formal one, in which the group might regularly take time to reflect on ways in which, collectively, norms are observed, as well as note the ways in which the group could improve or even revise its norms to better reflect current needs and values. For example, in our work, at the end of meetings, we would periodically take time to recognize the ways that individuals or the collective group carried out the norms, appreciating and applauding everyone's efforts. Reflecting on norms can also be impromptu, taking advantage of those moments that lend themselves to highlighting the ways in which norms are supporting the work, or, likewise, noting moments when staying true to a particular norm supported the group's process. In the latter case, it can be much more fruitful—and much less shaming—to refer back to a norm than to single out an individual who is not necessarily applying the norm.

Strategy 2: Use Resonant, Brief Examples as a Platform for Applying Relational Skills

Vignettes or case examples that feature relevant classroom experiences give educators a concrete (yet multifaceted) place to begin a conversation and provide a nonthreatening entry point to discussing difficult topics. We sometimes call them "resonant" examples to ensure that they are truly grounded in the everyday moments that make teaching and learning in early education challenging. These examples can be useful for supporting and enhancing all of the cornerstone educator competencies, but they are particularly useful for work focused on relational skills, because case examples offer an entryway into difficult conversations that address interpersonal interactions that might otherwise cause tension or frustration and be unproductive and/or hurtful. In our work with teachers, we have analyzed cases as a method for developing and refining relational skills, such as understanding the messages behind children's challenging behaviors; considering an opposing perspective in tense co-teaching situations (like that between Maria and Jada); and bringing common parent–educator misunderstandings to light. Figure 4.4 features two vignettes ripe for case analysis that we have written and used to spur conversations that focus on relational skills.

Writing Resonant Examples

The analysis of case examples is considered fundamental to teaching and learning in various disciplines (from the social sciences to law to medicine). When we designed our method for writing case examples and vignettes for use with early childhood educators, we drew on and tailored guidance from higher

---

Background: Ms. Sherri and Ms. Pam are preschool teachers at the Sunshine Early Education Center. Ms. Sherri has been teaching in the same classroom for 10 years. Ms. Pam started teaching at the Sunshine Center in September.

Case 1	Case 2
The children in Ms. Pam's and Ms. Sherri's class are excited about today's cultural festival. They have been working hard on the song they will sing to their parents and friends in the other classrooms. The children have been waiting anxiously all morning to be called by the director to come to the gym to perform. It is finally their turn, and they begin to walk to the door. Suddenly, from the back of the line a loud cry erupts. It is Max. Ms. Pam looks around and sees Max crying. She thinks, He has been looking forward to this for weeks! Why is he crying now? She says, "Max, stop! There is nothing to cry about!"	During center time, Ms. Sherri is helping a group of children with a painting project. She notices two other children arguing over blocks in the building corner. Ms. Sherri looks over at Ms. Pam. Ms. Sherri thinks that Ms. Pam sees the children arguing, but Ms. Pam continues working with children at the writing table. Ms. Sherri sighs and thinks to herself, Why doesn't she go over and help those children? Why do I always have to be the one to stop what I am doing and solve all the problems?

FIGURE 4.4. Sample vignettes for case analysis.

education and coupled it with our goal of using cases as platforms for applying cornerstone educator competencies—relational skills, in particular. You should feel free to use cases from this book for analysis with educators in your own school setting; you might also want to tweak them or even write your own case examples for analysis that embody your goals and closely match the lived experience of those in your setting. Here we list some useful steps to follow in writing these case examples.

1. Decide on a clear goal for the case study or vignette. What relational skill do you want educators to focus on and endeavor to apply? For example, when we presented Case 1 (see Figure 4.4)—featuring Max at a school cultural festival—our goal was to have teachers practice examining a child's perspective in difficult and/or charged situations, trying to understand the messages behind the child's behaviors.

2. Once you have your goal in mind, think of examples (perhaps from your own professional experiences) of classroom moments when educators would need to apply this relational skill. Examples usually involve an interpersonal dilemma—an emotionally charged or unpredictable, unexpected situation in which educators need to apply effective relational skills.

3. From these examples, pick one to write up that can be easily portrayed in a paragraph and will resonate most with educators in your group. While you want it to be familiar, do avoid writing a case that a group member will immediately recognize as happening in her classroom the week before!

4. Write the case. There is no need to be an expert writer to get this right. The point is just to capture a situation that will resonate with teachers—a moment or event that will feel very real to them. First, set the stage with the characters' names (fictitious), any important information about them (i.e., their roles at the early learning setting, their professional experience,), and

More Resources on Writing Case Examples

When designing this method for creating case examples, we primarily used guidance materials provided by:

- Carnegie Mellon University's Eberly Center for Teaching Excellence and Educational Innovation
- Vanderbilt University's Center for Teaching
- Brown University's Sheridan Center for Teaching and Learning

Visit these institutions' websites for more information.

the setting (where they work, the age of the children in their care, etc.). Then, describe the scene, leaving out your own commentary and analysis. *What are the characters doing and saying? What is happening around them?* It is preferable to leave some parts up to the imagination, thereby allowing your audience of educators to fill in some of the details themselves. Finally, have the case end in a way that underscores your conversation goals for using the case. Sometimes we end with a cliffhanger to really spark reaction and discussion. In Case 2, for example, the goal for the conversation was to practice taking the perspectives of co-teachers during tense classroom moments—so, at the end, we spell out that Ms. Sherri wishes her co-teacher had taken a different action. She is at a point when she could either jump to conclusions and let resentment build or find the energy and mind-set to take the constructive, problem-solving route with her colleague.

5. Write discussion questions and any follow-up activities to reflect your goal. Limit the number of questions you use to spark deep discussion. For example, we had three discussion questions for Case 1: Why might Max be crying when he had been so excited about going to the festival? How is Ms. Pam feeling? What questions do you have? As a follow-up activity, we brainstormed different reasons that children have meltdowns.

Putting Examples to Use

Whether you have written your own case example, or are using one from this book, how do you actually use it in the adult learning setting?

State the Goal. Be totally explicit about your goal for the analysis. For example, when we used Case 2, we stated that our goal was to understand the potential perspectives of the two teachers and consider how they might be feeling. We revisited previous conversations about emotion awareness and management strategies (see Chapter 3), and then introduced the idea that when emotions run high, perspective taking in the classroom can be difficult. We then explained that we were going to read a brief case and discuss what each of the teachers might have been thinking and feeling.

Read the Case or Vignette Aloud. We have found that doing this and then allowing group members some additional time for independent review accommodates educators' varying learning styles and literacy levels.

Use the Discussion Questions to Facilitate a Collaborative Case Analysis. The analysis stage is a critical moment to remind group members of key norms (i.e., sharing participation time) and to model them yourself (i.e., being

Zeroing In on Relationships in the Meeting
What to Do When Tensions Rise

To get this right in the classroom, we have to periodically focus our attention squarely on cultivating strong relationships among the educators participating in the regular staff meeting or the specific PLC. As the opening case for this chapter reveals, the busy early childhood classroom is ripe for misunderstandings and miscommunications, and as these miscommunications increase, tensions rise, and relationships suffer. When the atmosphere is stressful, it's easy to lay blame on the other adult. These same adults are those participating in professional development—and these same tensions will often also play out in the meeting, making it increasingly clear to the facilitator how difficult it is for educators to collaborate when relationships are under stress.

What can leaders, including facilitators and coaches, do when interactions are tense? Well, we found several strategies that helped teachers steer relationships toward more positive and constructive interactions. For example, periodically, we would ask group members to take time between meetings to fill out "compliment cards" about their colleagues. These cards featured a formal space for colleagues to tune in to one another's efforts and strengths and recognize and celebrate one another's hard work. Sometimes, coaching conferences (Chapter 8) were also used as a venue for addressing specific interpersonal difficulties. In these conversations, we might facilitate collaborative planning or problem solving between co-teachers or even role-play conflict management.

open to different points of view). The discussion can occur in a whole-group format, in smaller groups, or in pairs. In our work, we occasionally changed the seating arrangements so that participants engaged in case analyses with different group members. No matter what group format is used, be sure to encourage diverse perspectives and help participants use the case study to uncover their underlying assumptions. For example, when discussing the ways that Sherri could communicate with Pam about how she was feeling, several educators had the insight that, in a similar situation, they *would not* communicate with their colleague about their feelings at all. This insight gave us the opportunity to discuss why not, and then to think through strategies for having potentially uncomfortable or challenging conversations.

Bringing It All Together: Cultivating Strong Relationships in the Early Learning Setting

As educators and leaders in the early education field, we are committed to cultivating systems of strong relationships in the service of creating learning environments where educators do their best work and children thrive. Forging

PLCs in which group members apply, analyze, and reflect on relational skills and interpersonal dynamics is a huge step toward doing just that. But as we said earlier in this chapter—and it bears repeating—none of us are off the hook when it comes to mindfully cultivating and working hard to sustain strong relationships for the benefit of children's learning and development. It is up to each of us to consistently reflect on our own relational skills and interpersonal interactions in the early learning setting, seeking to understand others' points of view and to reach mutual understanding and collaboration. This work is never done, but the benefits for early learning settings are priceless. To that end, Figure 4.5 provides a self-study tool for leaders to use when reflecting on interpersonal interactions; use this tool to support your own insights into the ways in which relationships play out in your professional context and to plan the next steps in forging strong relationships with colleagues, staff, families, and children.

In the chapter that follows, we explore how educator talk—the language that early educators use throughout the day—is also a key lever for building classroom relationships and for positively influencing student learning outcomes.

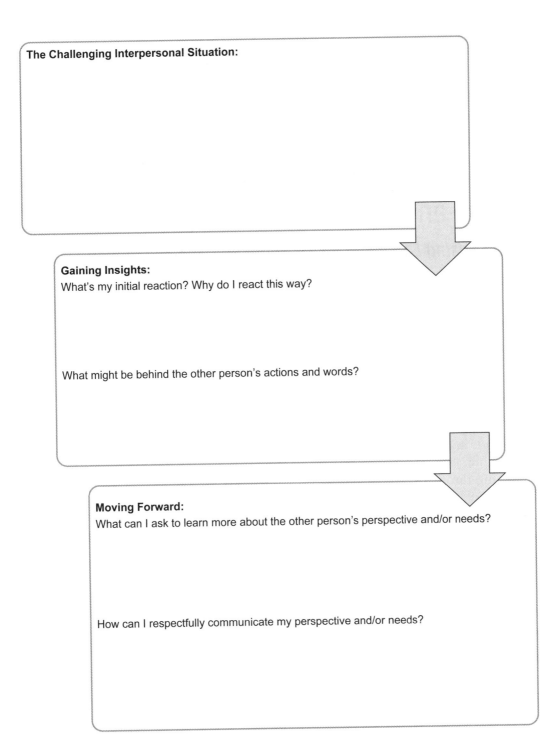

FIGURE 4.5. Relational reflection and planning tool.

From *The Early Education Leader's Guide* by Nonie K. Lesaux, Stephanie M. Jones, Annie Connors, and Robin Kane. Copyright © 2019 The Guilford Press. Permission to photocopy this figure is granted to purchasers of this book for personal use only (see copyright page for details). Purchasers can download an enlarged version of this figure (see the box at the end of the table of contents).

CHAPTER 5

Talk for Learning
and Classroom Management
Using Language for Learning and Self-Regulation

It is 9:30 at the Explorations Early Learning Center, and PreK teachers Jada and Maria are working to clean up breakfast so they can begin story time. Jada was able to stop by the library yesterday and, after searching through several titles, found a new book she thought the children would really enjoy. The cute little mouse in the story makes the most over-the-top facial expressions; once she saw the illustrations, Jada was sure her children would get a kick out of them. Leaving the library, she felt accomplished.

With the children settled on the rug, Jada reaches into her bag for the new book. Eager to get started, she nevertheless pauses to remind the children what the rules are for story time, asking everyone to sit criss-cross-applesauce, and to remember to raise a hand if they have something to say. Jada then holds the book up high, opens the cover, and gets ready to read, scanning the group. Although most of the children are sitting quietly waiting for Jada to start, Anthony and Mya are still talking, and Kylie is laying on her back instead of sitting as she should. Jada asks Anthony and Mya, "Do you want to lose your outside time today?" and asks Kylie, "Is that what we do on the carpet? We are not laying down right now." Anthony and Mya stop talking and turn to Jada, but Kylie is still lying down. "Do you need to leave the circle, Kylie?" Kylie shakes her head no and slowly sits up. By now, the other children are talking, and Jada tries to get their attention. She feels herself getting upset, but takes a breath and begins to read in a loud voice as the children quiet down and listen.

After reading through the book, from beginning to end, Jada asks the children "Who was the mouse hiding the strawberry from?" and "What color was the strawberry?" Jada is proud that the children know the answers to her questions and says to them, "Good job!" Then, Kylie calls out, "I love strawberries!" and Anthony shouts, "I'm not scared of bears!" Jada frowns and reminds them to raise a hand to speak. Feeling discouraged, Anthony hangs his head down, and when Mya puts her hand on his shoulder, Anthony slaps it away. Jada says, "Anthony! That wasn't nice. You need to leave the circle." Anthony shouts, "Fine. It's a dumb book anyway!"

Educators' talk—the words they use, and the ways in which they use them, whether teaching a lesson, reading a story, having a discussion with children, or even recounting the weekend—fills our early learning environments. Educators' talk shapes "classroom talk"—the daily talk that children are exposed to and participate in—that matters greatly for their later success. When educators use strategies to shape classroom talk in ways that bolster children's learning and cognitive and social–emotional development, they are engaging in *talk for learning*—the focus of this chapter.

How are *talk for learning* strategies playing out during the scene just described in Jada's classroom? To begin with, Jada reminds children of the expectations for story time (i.e., stating rules positively). She then engages children in a read-aloud (i.e., fosters interest in the world through joint reading). She also prompts some responses to the story when it is completed (i.e., uses questioning techniques to encourage participation). When it comes to talk for learning, Jada is on the right track. Of course, there are also many moments along the way in which Jada could have used additional talk for learning strategies—especially to get to deeper learning, which can also be a support for classroom management. In fact, by the end of story time, it is becoming clear that children are really hungry for *more* chances to talk, which is a good sign of their engagement with the story. As it happens, though, Jada perceives the developing excitement as misbehavior—and enthusiasm quickly turns to frustration. For Anthony, this results in yet another negative experience, not unlike the disappointment he endured in Chapter 3.

In this chapter, we delve deeply into classroom talk—what it is and what it looks like in high-quality early education settings. We explore the reasons why rich classroom talk is so important in the early years, and then outline four strategies for educators that enhance the quality of talk in their classrooms and that increase the amount of talking children do to promote their learning and development. We conclude the chapter with suggestions and tools for readers to use in supporting educators as they extend their use of talk for learning strategies.

What Is *Talk for Learning* and Why Does It Matter?

When educators intentionally use verbal (and nonverbal) communication to shape classroom talk in ways that stimulate conversations, build knowledge, and nurture relationships, they are engaging in what we call *talk for learning*. *Talk for learning* is essential for developing children's minds and relationships—it is a key ingredient for helping them acquire knowledge of the world and their connections to and identities within that world. It is through stimulating back-and-forth interactions—taking place in the context of strong relationships—that early language and reading skills are fostered, perspective taking develops, and critical thinking and mathematical reasoning are nurtured.

The substance and tone of educator's talk, and the degree to which children have the opportunity to participate in that talk, matter for children's learning—today and in the future (Bowers & Vasilyeva, 2011; Dickinson & Porche, 2011; Gámez & Levine, 2013; Huttenlocher, Vasilyeva, Cymerman, & Levine, 2002). In fact, when early educators engage in talk for learning, their impact on children's development has lasting effects. For example, we know that participation in high-quality preschool classroom talk continues to make a difference in children's reading achievement even by the time they reach fourth grade (Dickinson & Porche, 2011). And what we cannot leave out is that "talk" is the main mechanism through which educators build relationships with children and support them in building relationships with one another. In this sense, classroom talk—between educators and children, as well as among children—is what fuels social–emotional, literacy, and language learning.

Four Effective Strategies
for Bringing *Talk for Learning* into the Classroom

Getting to increased and effective talk for learning means regularly implementing four key strategies (see Figure 5.1). When educators engage in these strategies, they create the conditions necessary to cultivate learning environments that are at once cognitively stimulating and emotionally regulated. Let's take a look at each strategy and consider how Jada might use each one to enhance her classroom language environment.

Strategy 1: Using Books as Anchors

Listening to and talking about books help children learn about themselves and the world, all the while promoting their language and literacy development. As in Jada's classroom, joint reading is often already part and parcel of the

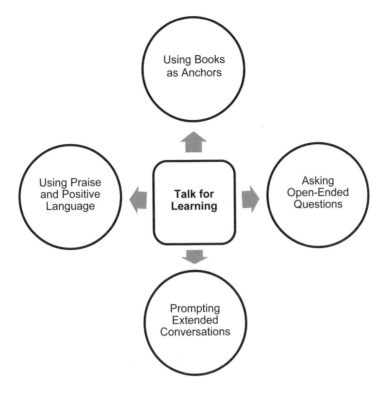

FIGURE 5.1. Four strategies to increase and enhance talk for learning in the classroom.

early childhood learning experience. Jada knows she can use books as a way to engage children and is aware that she can harness their interest by choosing a book with a likable character. But potential for engagement is just one element of a strong read-aloud choice: In the best cases, books are not only engaging, they are also connected to learning goals in the classroom. To take joint book reading to the next level—as a talk for learning strategy—we want to be sure that many of children's joint book reading experiences *anchor* learning. In that sense, books are chosen because they are engaging *and* because they are connected to the topics the class is studying. Therefore, an effective talk for learning strategy in the classroom revolves around sets of thematically related books to promote the accumulation of knowledge. In the best of cases, these thematically related books are part of a larger unit of study that frames joint book reading and supports the learning activities that occur throughout the day.

Most important, using books as anchors promotes lots of classroom talk—the book is not only anchoring content learning, it is also anchoring conversations! These conversations help children understand and think critically about the book's content. Because using books as anchors involves lots of classroom talk, this strategy is connected to and supports other key talk for learning strategies, including asking open-ended questions and engaging in extended conversations, which we discuss below. If we think back to Jada's classroom, she was definitely implementing this talk for learning strategy; she had spent some time the night before at the library searching for the right book, and she was thoughtful about whether it would engage the children. If we had to push back a little, we might ask whether the book's topic—the mouse that hid the strawberry—was connected in any way to other learning activities throughout the day and/or was embedded in a unit of study spanning multiple weeks.

Strategy 2: Asking Open-Ended Questions

Open-ended questions go beyond recall or one-word answers (the kinds of questions we often ask children). They can be answered in lots of different ways, and they encourage children to think more critically and offer more complex, elaborate responses. When we ask open-ended questions, we genuinely learn about and push on what children are thinking. We can ask these questions during joint book reading, center time, mealtime, or at the playground (just to name a few options!).

For these reasons, when we are considering Jada's questioning techniques, we want to encourage her to replace basic recall (i.e., "What color is the strawberry?") with open-ended questions that call for more than a one-word answer and instead result in a back-and-forth dialogue (i.e., "Why do you think the mouse was afraid?" or "Where would you hide the strawberry?"). To be sure, asking simple questions is a good and important way to begin a conversation and build confidence, especially for more reserved and introverted children. They also play a role in scaffolding learning. However, even when we do use them, we want to always be prioritizing open-ended questions, whether we are discussing a book, guiding classroom play, or supporting children to put words to difficult emotions. Strong open-ended questions are

- designed to prompt children's thinking and discussion about classroom learning (i.e., thematic unit of study), and
- incite extended conversations (Strategy 3, described in the next section).

Strategy 3: Prompting Extended Conversations

When educators prompt extended conversations—either with one child or among a group of children—they are building on children's thoughts, feelings, and experiences, as well as asking questions that matter greatly for learning and development (Epstein, 2014). What do we mean by an extended conversation? This type of classroom conversation

- involves multiple turns for each speaker.
- expands on children's talk about the present moment (i.e., the here and now) to ideas, events, and possibilities in the past and future.
- sounds like a story or explanation (not a series of questions or directions).

Prompting extended conversations often begins with an open-ended question (Strategy 2), but we should not seek out one child's response and then move on to another question. Instead, these conversations go back and forth (and back and forth again!), frequently including multiple children's thoughts and perspectives. During extended conversations, the educator is often "actively listening"—fully engaging with children's thoughts and experiences, without judging them, and helping children to feel understood, heard, and supported. She is also turning over the talk to children to encourage more participation, rather than just asking questions of each of them. So, for example, Jada might:

- use a conversation routine (i.e., "turn and talk" or "think–pair–share") to support young children to have extended conversations. For instance, after asking children "Why do you think the mouse was afraid?", she might then have children turn and talk with one another about their ideas. She would then circulate among several pairs, supporting and encouraging back-and-forth talk.
- plan a follow-up activity that prompts extended conversations. For example, still using the book as an anchor (Strategy 1), children might act out the story in the dramatic play area during learning centers. Jada could guide this play, prompting children to discuss together how best to hide the strawberry from the hungry bear.

Strategy 4: Using Praise and Positive Language

When educators use praise as a talk for learning strategy, they are:

- genuinely and explicitly labeling and encouraging children's efforts, and
- supporting children to encourage and praise one another.

In all cases, this kind of praise helps set the stage for children to develop positive perceptions of themselves and others (Meece & Soderman, 2010). While some forms of praise might have the unintended consequence of fostering children's dependence on the judgments of others to feel good about themselves, when praise encourages specific efforts (rather than focusing on accomplishments or competition), it has the potential to instill an internal sense of confidence and competence. For this reason, educators should not wait for behavior to be perfect before offering praise! Thinking back to the case of Jada, by singling out Anthony and Mya with a negative, rhetorical question (i.e., "Do you want to lose your outside time today?"), she missed the opportunity to instead offer specific praise to the many children on the carpet who were observing story time expectations. Doing so would have nurtured those behaviors, while simultaneously offering Anthony and Mya an additional cue to turn their attention to the reading activity.

Positive language, like praise, is constructive and specific. Educators use positive language when they

- state expectations and redirect children in ways that make clear what they should do and why (i.e., "When we are quiet during a story and make space for everyone on the carpet, we can all do our best learning), rather than focusing on what they should not do (i.e., "Is that what we do on the carpet? We are not laying down right now.").
- communicate to children (verbally and nonverbally) that they respect and value them as individuals and as members of the classroom community. That means, for example, expressing interest in what they have to say, validating their emotions and perceptions, and supporting children to view and treat their peers positively.

What Does *Talk for Learning* Have to Do with Classroom Management?

Effective classroom management involves implementing all the structures and steps that go into a calm, smoothly run, and prosocial learning environment—a classroom in which children have internalized the routines and expectations. Typically when educators talk and think about classroom management, they focus on classroom organization, schedules, rules, and routines (Harms, Cryer, & Clifford, 2003; Raver et al., 2009), such as setting up and maintaining

- the physical environment and materials in ways that are well organized for learning;
- a daily schedule that supports children to move easily through personal-care routines (i.e., hand washing, mealtime, nap time) and learning activities (i.e., circle time, learning centers);
- transition routines that are quick and often include a purposeful activity (particularly during wait time);

- expectations for children's behaviors, made clear through ongoing communication, visual aids, and monitoring;
- systems for children to collaborate (i.e., turn-taking routines) and for conflict management (i.e., strategies for dealing with anger and disappointment, go-to places for children to work through problems and visual aids to support children as they learn and use the calm-down strategies); and
- routines for encouraging and supporting child choice and initiative (i.e., a choice board for activities).

So, how is talk for learning connected to this classroom management work? In other words, why would the talk for learning strategies we describe here (i.e., prompting extended conversations; using books as anchors) not only support children's learning, but also support effective classroom management? Research has found that the words educators use and the opportunities that educators give children to talk influence children's behaviors, interactions, and relationships—all of which are crucial for a smooth-running and emotionally regulated classroom! Executing classroom management strategies effectively involves using high-quality language. By extension, using high-quality language leads to fewer challenges with classroom management.

In other words, talk for learning strategies have a reciprocal relationship with classroom management (see Figure 5.2). How does this work? Well,

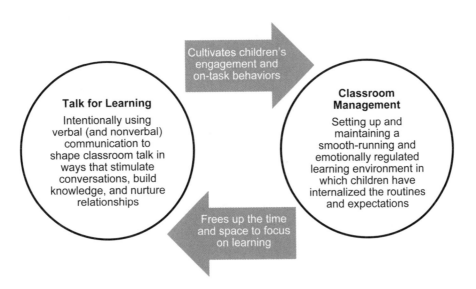

FIGURE 5.2. The relationship between talk for learning strategies and classroom management.

children are more likely to stay on task and avoid problem behaviors when they are actively engaged in their learning environment (i.e., participating through talk) and when their efforts are encouraged and praised; and, likewise, effective classroom management strategies make the use of talk for learning strategies even more productive, because well-managed classrooms—classrooms that are socially and emotionally regulated—free up educators and children to focus on the learning activities. Actually, in many cases, these strategies and classroom management strategies are one and the same (see Table 5.1).

TABLE 5.1. Talk for Learning: Classroom Talk That Supports Management and Learning

Use *talk for learning* strategies to . . .	What might this look like?	How do these strategies simultaneously support learning and classroom management?
. . . make learning activities interactive	• In whole class or small group, children engage in extended conversations about what they are learning, doing, and thinking.	• Extended conversations are more engaging than many other interactions (e.g., listening while one child responds), and therefore children are more likely to stay focused on the task at hand.
. . . embed planned play and talk into daily routines	• Centers are organized around purposeful play; mealtime includes content-rich conversations, and wait time includes talk (i.e., children are talking, singing, or rhyming when lining up or waiting for the next activity).	• Children are learning throughout the day—even during "noninstructional" time—and the inappropriate behaviors that come with too much idle wait time are diminished.
. . . encourage children's efforts toward contributing to a smooth-running and emotionally supportive classroom community	• Children receive frequent and specific positive feedback and encouragement when they are engaged, following directions, and demonstrating effort and progress. • Classroom expectations and rules are co-created with children, and they are prompted to recall and observe them before being redirected (e.g., Can anyone tell me one way that we can all make it easier for everyone to see the book?)	• Specific praise helps children to learn classroom expectations and supports them to view and treat their peers positively. • When children are part of the process of creating the classroom conditions, they are engaging in important language-building conversations, and they are more likely to internalize and follow these expectations.

What Tools Can We Use to Support
Early Educators' Use of *Talk for Learning* Strategies?

Tool 1: Use Resonant, Brief Case Examples as a Platform
for Analyzing *Talk for Learning* Strategies

As we discussed in Chapter 4, case examples that feature relevant classroom experiences give educators a concrete (and yet multifaceted) place to begin a conversation. Case examples can be useful for supporting and enhancing talk for learning strategies because they allow educators to "see" these strategies in action and to discuss classroom talk in a group format. In our own work facilitating PLCs among early educators, we focused on enhancing cornerstone educator competencies. After establishing group norms (see Chapter 4), we spent the first set of sessions examining talk for learning strategies. Because these strategies are foundational to the stimulating and nurturing classroom environment, our goals were to inform teachers about these best practices, increase self-awareness regarding how they are used in participants' classrooms, and crucially, to commit—as a PLC—to working on making these strategies part of teaching every day. We posted these strategies next to our group norms so that we could refer back to them throughout our PLC work. When introducing each strategy, we

1. discussed what, exactly, it is,
2. analyzed a classroom case featuring the strategy, and
3. made an initial plan for how to apply the strategy.

We found that in our work with some educators that this was the first time they considered some of these strategies (for example, some teachers did not regularly engage in supporting their preschoolers to have back-and-forth conversations); for other educators, these strategies were very familiar. What we were sure to reinforce was that the launch of this learning community was an opportunity to take these strategies to the next level, no matter one's starting point. As an example, Figure 5.3 features the case example, discussion questions, and follow-up activity we employed to engage educators in dialogue about the talk for learning Strategy 4, *using praise and positive language*. For suggestions on how to design your own case examples, taking your particular classroom context and goals into account, see Chapter 4.

Tool 2: Use *Talk for Learning* Strategies as the Platform for Applying
Other Cornerstone Competencies in PLCs

We can support early educators' use of talk for learning strategies by embedding the application of these strategies in our efforts to address the other

Case

It is time to go to the gym. Ms. Pam knows that some children have a difficult time stopping what they are doing to line up. Other children become overexcited about going to the gym and can't seem to stand in line without bumping into their classmates and knocking them over. Keeping this in mind, Ms. Pam gives the class a 5-minute warning, after which, she tells them, they will use calm bodies and walking feet to line up at the door to go to gym. As she calls the children to line up, Ms. Pam notices that the line is not perfect and that there are still a couple of children who have not yet lined up, but she still makes a point of smiling at the children and saying, "Class, I noticed how you stopped what you were doing and listened to the directions about lining up." She smiles again. "It helps us get to the gym on time when everyone lines up quickly."

Discussion Questions

- In what ways is Ms. Pam using praise to help children understand what she expects them to do during this time?

- How is Ms. Pam using praise to recognize that children are making an effort to follow the rules?

What I Can Do: Two Ways to Name and Praise Positive Behavior

- I noticed that _____ made a safe choice when _____.

- _____, I noticed that you _____. That's _____.

FIGURE 5.3. Sample case and discussion activities for talk for learning strategy: Use praise and positive language.

cornerstone educator competencies (see Figure 5.4, introduced in Chapter 1 as Figure 1.3). After all, when educators are applying their EF strategies by planning and reflecting, they need some substance in their plans and a focus for their reflections. Similarly, when educators are working on emotion regulation and relational competencies in the classroom, they are necessarily working on the nature of the talk they engage in when managing emotions and nurturing relationships—how they use books, conversations, and praise and positive language to support a high-quality social–emotional learning environment.

Let's consider an example to shed further light on how to use talk for learning strategies as the platform for applying other cornerstone competencies. In

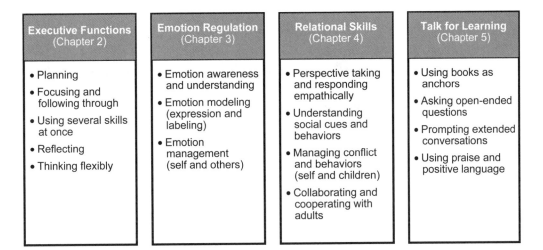

FIGURE 5.4. Recap: Cornerstone educator competencies.

our work with educators, we regularly focus on using high-quality children's literature in classrooms so that educators could engage in the first talk for learning strategy, *using books as anchors*. But also, to support emotion regulation and relational skills in the classroom, a criterion for the books we chose was that they served as anchors for supporting educators' talk around labeling emotions, managing emotions and behaviors, managing conflict, and building relationships. Figure 5.5 lists some of the children's literature we selected.

Of course, we did not just select and supply the books and leave it at that. Just as educators use books as anchors for learning, we used these books as anchors for our work in the PLC. As a group, we would first unpack the book—we discussed the social–emotional learning goals associated with the book and co-teachers would use a planning tool (see Chapter 2) to prepare for the joint-reading activity, including the design of an open-ended question that corresponded with the book and learning goals. Thus, teachers were applying their executive functioning (i.e., planning) *and* their relational skills (i.e., collaborating) in order to implement strong talk for learning in the classroom.

However, the work of enhancing these educator competencies did not stop there. Our PLC meetings always built on what participants accomplished in the previous one, and so at our next meeting, we would reflect (another key EF skill!) on the joint-reading experiences educators engaged in with children. Reflection questions might orient the conversation around educators' use of any number of cornerstone educator competencies, such as their use of books as anchors, modeling and labeling emotions, collaborating in the teaching process, or reflecting on the plan itself. We then would apply relational skills,

---

Labeling Emotions

On Monday When It Rained by Cherryl Kachenmeister

Today I Feel Silly & Other Moods That Make My Day by Jamie Lee Curtis and Laura Cornell

The Mixed-Up Chameleon by Eric Carle

Managing Emotions and Behaviors

Sometimes I'm Bombaloo by Rachel Vail and Yumi Heo

How Do Dinosaurs Go to School? by Jane Yolen

Managing Conflict and Building Relationships

How Full Is Your Bucket? by Tom Rath, Mary Reckmeyer, and Maurie J. Manning

A Weekend with Wendell by Kevin Henkes

Matthew and Tilly by Rebecca C. Jones

For more great book recommendations, check out the Center on the Social and Emotional Foundations for Early Learning booklist: *http://csefel.vanderbilt.edu/*.

FIGURE 5.5. Using anchor books as platforms for social–emotional learning and talk for learning.

collaboratively planning a follow-up lesson and activity, which would most often involve rereading the book and engaging in extended conversations, frequently incorporating a conversation routine, such as think–pair–share, into the plan. This follow-up planning might also include opportunities to apply EF skills, such as forecasting potential difficulties and designing strategies for addressing these pitfalls.

Bringing It All Together: Leading for High-Quality Language Environments

We know that preparing and supporting early educators to effectively use talk for learning strategies are crucial ways in which early education leaders can cultivate regulated and rigorous learning environments. After all, educators draw on these strategies to shape classroom talk so that it makes a big difference for children's learning, positive identity, and relationships. So, how can we lead our learning environments in a manner that promotes the use of these strategies? Well, as with the other cornerstone educator competencies, it takes a leadership approach that is *self-reflective* and *process oriented*.

By *self-reflective,* we mean that leaders must consider how they model talk for learning strategies, carefully thinking about how they are shaping educators' language environments. For example, are praise and positive language part of everyday interactions with adults and children? Are extended conversations, characterized by active listening and the inclusion of multiple voices, commonplace? Likewise, it is important to reflect on the messages we are sending educators about classroom talk, either explicitly or implicitly. For example, do we (erroneously) label classrooms as "regulated" when they are actually most often quiet and the emphasis is on behavioral compliance? Do we (erroneously) interpret instruction as "rigorous" when learning opportunities involve lots of teacher talk and minimal child talk? Educators need to feel free—and encouraged!—to regularly take the risk of providing children with learning opportunities that make for noisier, more boisterous classrooms, and they need encouragement in promoting this kind of complex, interaction-based learning.

By *process-oriented,* we mean that leaders recognize that enhancing talk for learning strategies does not happen overnight. It takes hard work and ongoing professional development to continually fine-tune and master these strategies. As such, leading classroom settings characterized by high-quality language environments means conducting ongoing professional development that honors what we know about adult learning and change.

Bearing in mind the complex—but incredibly exciting and fruitful—process of adult learning and change, Part II of this book focuses on the professional development structures that promote learning and teaching. We begin by discussing the ways in which a new model of workforce development must ultimately replace the widespread, yet outdated, model of one-off off-site trainings that are insufficient to bring about changes in everyday practice. We then dig into a process-oriented approach to staff development that is intensive, data-driven, collaborative, and linked to practice.

Before we turn to the professional development strategies that promote learning and teaching in Chapter 6, we encourage your use of the self-study tool featured in Figure 5.6 to reflect on the ways in which early educators' effective talk for learning strategies are supported in your educational setting.

Talk for Learning Strategies Early Educators Have and Use	*What, exactly, is this strategy?*	*How do we support early educators' use of this strategy? (e.g., modeling its use daily, providing necessary materials, facilitating practice through professional development)*	*What else might we do to further support early educators' use of this strategy?*
Using books as anchors	• Reading and discussing books that are connected to classroom learning and support children's knowledge development		
Asking open-ended questions	• Posing questions that require elaborate responses, don't have one "right" answer, and incite conversation		
Prompting extended conversations	• Supporting conversations with and among children that go back and forth, go outside of the here and now and into the abstract, and sound like a story or explanation		
Using praise and positive language	• Labeling and encouraging children's efforts • Supporting children to encourage and praise one another • Explaining what children should do and why • Communicating to children that they are respected and valued		

FIGURE 5.6. Self-study: Reflecting on effective talk for learning strategies.

PART II

Professional Development That Promotes and Supports Educator Competencies

CHAPTER 6

Designing Effective Professional Development

After seeing the last child off, Melinda, the director of the Explorations Early Learning Center, sits down at her desk and turns back to her quality rating report, a self-assessment that is due at the end of the week. Melinda's mind is churning; she is at a loss to explain why scores on their formal classroom observation tool continue to show that the quality of instructional support in nearly all of the classrooms is low, and why there is so much variation among her teachers in the domain of emotional support. She has been focused with her staff on the features of a high-quality learning environment—the classroom conversations and warm responsive interactions—for months now, and the teachers at the Center are up to date on their professional development hours. In fact, from her records, Melinda sees that her teachers have all exceeded the required 20 hours of training per year.

Recently, Jada, in the PreK room, attended a half-day workshop called Give Them Something to Talk About at the local community college. Her co-teacher, Maria, went to one of the trainings advertised on the flyer they receive each month from the state; this training was about creative thinking in the classroom, and Melinda heard from Maria that the presenters showed very interesting examples of student work that gave her ideas for a series of classroom projects. Melinda saw readily how these projects could get children talking eagerly and engaged in positive interactions. Plus, in preparation for the classroom observations, Melinda sent all of the teachers at the Center a webinar about leading classroom discussions. Puzzled, Melinda thinks to herself: Why don't the teachers apply what they are learning from all these trainings?

Melinda is confronting a challenge that so many leaders in early education face: how to ensure that educators are provided with learning opportunities that translate into meaningful improvements in classroom practices. It is clear that Melinda is working hard to meet this challenge thoughtfully and purposefully; she is looking at data to understand the needs at her site, communicating with teachers about those needs, and ensuring that educators attend professional development offerings. But there are changes that Melinda could make to her leadership strategy that would sharpen her approach and result in significant boosts in the quality of the classroom learning environments at the Center. Her struggles are common—and there is little guidance for leaders like Melinda to draw on when devising a professional development plan that truly shifts practice.

In this chapter, we describe what it takes to promote meaningful learning among educators. We delve into three key components of a model for 21st-century adult learning, provide self-study tools leaders can use to analyze their current approaches to professional development, and conclude by offering some guidance on how to switch to this newer, more effective model.

From Traditional Training to a 21st-Century Adult Learning Model

All too often, reform efforts fail to effect lasting changes because they attend insufficiently to the adult skills and knowledge necessary for **making the transition from professional training to changes in practice**. To be sure, the issue is not that early educators have not received or participated in in-service training. Like the teachers at the Explorations Early Learning Center, where Melinda is grappling with getting to meaningful improvement, early educators across the nation do participate in professional learning offerings. But in today's context, where there are unparalleled expectations for what early education, and thus early educators, must accomplish for all children, the traditional training models are not going to meet these expectations (Phillips, 2016). There is a mismatch, a gaping chasm even, between the nature of today's professional development for early educators and the impact on practice that we expect those experiences to deliver.

But, there *is* good news. Insights from emerging research show that strong professional learning can have the impact on practice that leaders desire and that educators deserve. Here we synthesize insights from recent research (Darling-Hammond, Wei, & Johnson, 2009; Neuman & Cunningham, 2009; Zaslow, Martinez-Beck, Tout, & Halle, 2011), scholarship (Lieberman & Miller, 2014) and our own research and professional partnerships; together, these insights alter traditional conceptions of professional development toward what we are calling a 21st-century model of adult learning. Figure 6.1 outlines these shifts.

Components of a 21st-Century Model of Adult Learning

In the sections that follow, and as outlined in Figure 6.2, we focus on the core components of this 21st-century model of adult learning in a way that helps the leader put this new model into practice. It is important to notice that the components are interrelated—together they create powerful opportunities to enhance learning and teaching.

Component 1: Intensive

Although many early educators attend professional development sessions, these trainings are typically infrequent, one-off, and extremely short in duration (i.e., one half day), and, further, the topics they cover do not clearly connect to one another. Given this design, even when educators do accrue the required professional-development hours, they often do not translate into enhanced practice. If professional learning is going to enhance educator skills and competencies, and in turn change long-held beliefs and entrenched behaviors, the format has to be sufficiently intensive (Zaslow, Tout, Halle, Whittaker, & Lavelle, 2010). By *intensive* (see Figure 6.3), we mean that professional

Traditional Training	21st-Century Model
Sessions consist of infrequent, one-off trainings that are typically extremely short in duration (e.g., a half day) and are focused on discrete, isolated topics and strategies.	Frequent, ongoing, and cohesive professional learning opportunities are the norm.
Topics of focus are of general interest based on educational fads, the latest policy updates, or on arbitrary (but available) outside training offerings.	Learning opportunities are directly related to site-level needs and improvement plans based on data.
Sessions are organized such that educators are passive participants and their learning is compromised.	Sessions are interactive, and educator collaboration is integral.
Educators take ideas learned during a session and then strive (and often struggle) to put new practices into action without classroom supports or follow-up.	Both group-based sessions *and* postgroup session supports that facilitate and scaffold classroom applications are involved.

FIGURE 6.1. Transforming professional development for 21st-century adult learning.

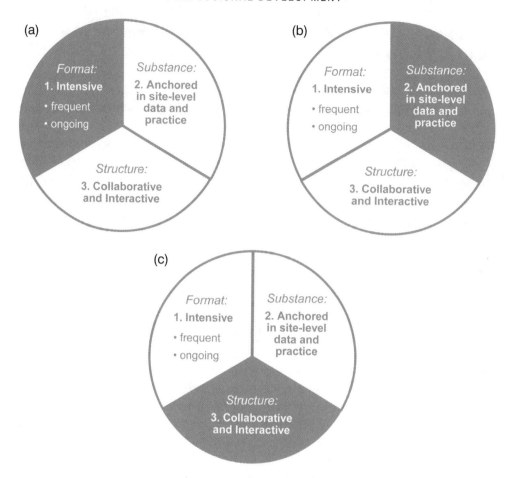

FIGURE 6.2. Key strategies for designing effective professional development.

- Raise awareness of competencies and practices
- Support implementation of specific procedures

- Enhance competencies and practices
- Support classroom processes and interactions

Intensity

frequency, duration, cohesion

FIGURE 6.3. Professional development: A design continuum.

development should involve learning opportunities that are *frequent and ongoing* (i.e., part of a long-term learning plan), as well as *cohesive* (i.e., connections are made from one session to the next).

To be sure, less-intensive learning opportunities do have their place in the professional lives of educators. For example, they can serve to raise awareness about particular practices or available resources—perhaps even kick off a site-based improvement strategy. They might also be effective for troubleshooting the implementation of a specific, concrete procedure or strategy that a group of educators have been working on. However, when our goal is to fundamentally enhance the quality of early learning environments—for example, targeting the educator competencies described in Part I of this book—we must turn to a 21st-century model that features intensive learning opportunities.

As a leader, consider the professional learning opportunities in which your educators participate. How do their learning experiences hold up against the design presented in Figure 6.3? Are learning experiences frequent, ongoing, *and* cohesive? Use the self-study questions and corresponding rating scales presented in Figure 6.4 to guide your analysis.

Elements of Intensity	Intensity Rating
Frequency: How frequent are professional development opportunities?	One-off sessions　　　　　Frequent sessions ● ● ● ● ●
Duration: Over what period of time do we maintain focus on a particular focus?	Brief　　　　　Ongoing ● ● ● ● ●
Cohesion: Are learning opportunities cohesive? Do they connect from one to the next, building off of each other?	Disconnected　　　　　Interrelated ● ● ● ● ●

FIGURE 6.4. Self-study tool for the intensity of professional development.

Based on this self-study, we encourage leaders to identify the ways in which their current approach is sufficiently intensive, as well as the ways in which learning opportunities could be ratcheted up for deeper learning. For example, perhaps they are *frequent,* but they are not connected to each other over time—and therefore together they do not represent a *cohesive* approach. Or, perhaps the approach is *cohesive,* that is, learning opportunities focus on one aspect of practice or a specific educator skill or competency, but they are typically too brief or infrequent for new knowledge to take hold in actual classrooms.

Whatever the case may be, once a leader has identified the aspect(s) of the approach to supporting educator learning that is not sufficiently intensive, the first step is to consider what it might take to alter the approach in ways that will result in accumulated learning and improved practice. We recognize that this is easier said than done. Creating an intensive plan might require capitalizing on adult-learning structures that already exist but using them in a new way; it might also require adopting new adult-learning structures or policies. What is important to consider is that research on professional development for early educators converges on the notion that learning *about* a practice, and successfully putting that practice *into action,* are not one and the same (Zaslow et al., 2010, 2011). Educators need support as they take new ideas from professional development sessions and implement them in their settings—and the plan needs to take this into account. To achieve palpable shifts in the quality of learning environments and children's outcomes, supports need to be in place to facilitate the link between professional learning and actual practice.

Thinking back again to Melinda's frustration in this chapter's opening vignette, tightening the link between professional learning and everyday practice might be one of the highest-lever strategies for improvement at the Explorations Early Learning Center. For example, as it now stands, Jada, Maria, and their colleagues at the Center are participating in professional development, but there are no existing structures or processes that make them cohesive and that link them to their everyday practice. For these reasons, in subsequent chapters, we discuss professional learning communities (PLCs) and connected coaching (CC)—two structures that lend themselves to intensive professional learning.

Component 2: Data-Driven

The second step in achieving professional development that better suits the work of early educators on the ground involves avoiding the all-too-common practice of making decisions about topics for professional learning based on general interest, educational fads, or what is available or offered locally.

Instead, designing a plan that tightly links professional-learning opportunities with genuine professional learning needs is a powerful step toward creating the conditions educators require to cultivate high-quality learning environments. And, thankfully, whether a leader is working at the state, center, or classroom level, a valuable resource is already available in abundance that can help address the question "What, exactly, are my site's needs?" That resource is data.

In the vignette presented in the chapter's opening, we saw just how useful data can be. Melinda, the Center director, used the results from ongoing classroom observations to identify several site-level needs. In her case, classroom discussions were not common, and some classrooms were not as supportive and emotionally responsive as they should be. While each state, district, and/or center might gather information that is different from Melinda's data, one thing is for sure: Throughout the early education and care system, unprecedented amounts of data are gathered day to day and year to year.

Unfortunately, despite the significant time invested in gathering data, the information rarely gets used in ways that go beyond compliance. And yet, the information collected can and should inform improvement efforts, including professional development planning. For many, the question is: How to go about using the data productively? Even in the case of Melinda, there are ways in which she could further use the information she possesses to identify and design strategic goals for the Explorations Early Learning Center. In the next part of the chapter, we describe how to put the data to good use, working through three steps for figuring out data-driven goals for educators' professional learning (see Figure 6.5).

Step 1: Take Stock of Available Data

Using data to inform professional learning goals requires that we understand the data we have—the categories (or types) of data gathered and the kinds of information these data capture. Broadly, there are four categories of data that many of today's early educators and early education leaders are continually collecting. Each of these types of data captures different kinds of information.

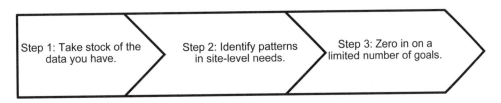

FIGURE 6.5. Steps for a data-driven professional learning plan.

• *Formal child assessments.* These data shed light on children's learning and development across domains (e.g., language, literacy, social–emotional). Often, these data are gathered to identify whether a child is at risk in a particular developmental domain. Example assessments that provide data in this category include Ages & Stages Questionnaires® and Teaching Strategies GOLDplus™.

• *Assessments of classroom practices and quality.* These data are usually gathered through observation. They capture the nature of classroom interactions, instruction, and organization. Example assessments that provide data in this category include the Early Language and Literacy Classroom Observation (ELLCO) tool, the Early Childhood Environment Rating Scale (ECERS), and the Classroom Assessment Scoring System™ (CLASS).

• *Assessments of setting-level quality.* These data are often required for licensing, for accreditation, and for qualifying for the Quality Rating and Improvement System (QRIS). They often include self-assessments, outside observations, and document review. Together, these assessments capture a wide range of practices and procedures implemented in an early childhood setting, including curriculum approaches, health and safety routines, workforce qualifications and training, family and community engagement practices, and leadership quality.

• *Incident reports and daily logs.* From attendance and learning to meals and toothbrushing, early educators are tasked with logging and recording a lot of data. These data are immensely important to families and are necessary for compliance purposes. But to be sure, incident reports (i.e., illness, injury, or behavior) and daily logs documenting health and safety routines also provide very valuable information for identifying site-level needs.

To support the self-study of data available to you in your setting—the types of data gathered and the information that can be learned from them—use the chart in Figure 6.6.

Step 2: Identify Patterns in Site-Level Data

In this step the leader analyzes the available data with an eye toward areas for growth and improvement. The key here is to look for specific *patterns* and *trends* at scale and to avoid two common pitfalls:

• Focusing on singular, but highly salient, examples of difficulties (i.e., Anthony struggles to control his emotional outbursts and has had several incidents when he nearly injured others); and/or
• Making broad, rather than targeted, assumptions (i.e., the Green Room has a difficult group of children this year).

Data Categories	What do we use to collect these data?	What can I learn about my setting from this information?
Formal child assessments		
Assessments of classroom practices and quality		
Assessments of setting-level quality		
Incident reports and daily logs		

FIGURE 6.6. Self-study tool for taking stock of the data you have.

The kind of individualized problem solving that is referenced as the first pitfall should happen only *after* trends in the classroom's overall data have been identified. After all, sometimes the most salient difficulties are simply an indicator of a challenge that is affecting many more children than the one who is most visible. The second pitfall—the sweeping assumption about a classroom—is to be avoided because identifying patterns in data often shows that descriptors like "always" and "constantly" are not usually accurate and tend to lead us to think they cannot be changed. Instead, there are more specific patterns or particular triggers for difficulties, which have likely not been identified as yet, that could be the target of a change process.

Identifying patterns in site-level needs requires that early education leaders review the information on hand, both within data categories and across these categories. As data are reviewed, it is important for leaders to be open to the many different needs that may be uncovered and to pay particular attention to questions that relate to

- *Learning and engagement* (i.e., What domains of development present difficulties for the majority of children in my context? What times of day are talk for learning strategies often employed, and when are they lacking?)
- *Relationships* (i.e., What do I notice about how children treat one another? What do I notice about teacher–child interactions? What do I notice about staff collaboration?)
- *Stability* (i.e., What routines are working, what routines are not used consistently and/or are not working, and when are routines missing? What parts of the day seem chaotic for children and teachers?)
- *Hot spots* (i.e., What times of day do incidents typically arise? What kinds of situations seem to lead to hard-to-manage levels of classroom stress?)

We encourage leaders to use the form in Figure 6.7 to record patterns and trends.

Step 3: Zero In on a Very Limited Number of Goals

For a professional learning plan to be effective, it has to be designed around specific, articulated goals (Zaslow et al., 2010). Therefore, this third step requires that early education leaders look at identified patterns in data and translate those patterns into specific goals. At this stage, prioritization is crucial. That is to say, having surfaced patterns in the data, many potential goals are likely to emerge. But if a professional learning plan is organized around too

Review data	What do you notice?
Formal child assessments	
Assessments of classroom practices and quality	
Assessments of setting-level quality	
Incident reports and daily logs	

Looking across data categories, what patterns do you notice?

FIGURE 6.7. Self-study tool for identifying patterns in site-level needs.

When It's Not about Professional Development
Surfacing a Problematic Procedure or Policy

After taking a sip of the now tepid coffee on her desk, Melinda reaches for the binder of daily logs, flipping through the pages of this month's Incident and Injury Report. She recalls signing off on most, but hadn't yet reviewed them together. Now, she sees a pattern: A majority of the behavior incidents and injuries occurred following afternoon snack, between 3:30 and 4:00 P.M. She pauses, and then realizes that a staffing change occurs at this time. Some of her staff leaves, and so either the Busy Bee and Butterfly rooms are combined, or a floating teacher is sent into one room and a teacher is pulled from a low-attendance room to cover the other. It looks like several children demonstrate aggressive behavior during these transitions, and this happens regularly. She can hear the teachers in these two classrooms venting to her, "Our children act out all the time," and she nearly laughs to herself. "Yes, they act out all the time," she thinks. "All the time between 3:30 and 4:00."

By analyzing patterns across incident and injury reports, Melinda arrives at a very important conclusion: a Center policy is creating unnecessary and overly taxing instability, leading to difficulties for children and teachers. In this instance, designing a professional development plan around the goal, for example, of preventing and deescalating challenging behaviors would not address the root cause of the issue. Instead, Melinda needs to revisit her site's complex and sometimes unpredictable staffing practices in order to devise a strategy that restores stability and predictability.

many goals, educators will only be able to scratch the surface of any particular topic—in turn, depth of learning will be compromised and any change in practice is unlikely. A solid plan is guided by one, maybe two, goals.

When prioritizing, it may be helpful for leaders to look at a list of potential goals and identify those "power goals" that may accomplish several objectives at once (in other words, they have a lot of bang for the buck), and therefore make a big difference in the *quality* of learning environments, while reducing issues in the domain of health and safety. For example, perhaps early educators in a particular setting report that transitions are particularly stressful at certain times of day, and, in fact, daily logs indicate that incidents are most common when children are waiting for extended lengths of time (e.g., waiting in line to wash their hands, waiting for meals to be served, waiting to be called on to visit stations, center, or the movement room down the hall). At the same time, perhaps formal child assessments indicate that many children demonstrate underdeveloped vocabulary. When considering these issues together, one could imagine a plan organized around a power goal of introducing engaging activities into daily transitions to both increase the speed of the transitions and enhance daily language-learning opportunities. There is potential for significant positive change, for both children and teachers, when data are used to zero in on and target a site's highest priorities.

Component 3: Collaborative and Interactive

Having addressed the format (*intensive*) and the substance (*data-driven*) components, we now turn our attention to the structure used to engage educators in professional learning. What kinds of learning experiences facilitate sustained behavior change? Well, it is clear that a 21st-century approach to professional learning must be collaborative and interactive. In other words, effective professional opportunities involve the frequent buzz of discussion and dialogue; they provide educators with ongoing opportunities to work together with colleagues toward joint learning and collective problem solving (Darling-Hammond et al., 2009).

Why focus on collaboration and interaction? There are actually many reasons why educator collaboration in an interactive professional learning environment matters, especially when teams (working in the same setting or collaborating to meet the learning needs of the same children) participate together (Zaslow et al., 2010). Collaboration and interaction promote

• *Educator learning.* Learning, by its very nature, is social. When educators are given frequent opportunities to talk ideas through and share insights about their own learning, rather than just reading or listening to learn, knowledge is deepened and misunderstandings are both brought to light and clarified.

• *Instructional consistency.* When professional learning supports and encourages collaboration and interaction among educators working in the same setting, educators have formal opportunities to communicate with one another about *how* they are implementing a particular approach or strategy and can share their unique content, instructional, and experiential expertise. These professional conversations can shift instruction in separate classrooms toward a converged set of the most effective practices, such that children receive comparably strong learning experiences across classrooms in the same building.

• *Strengthened professional relationships.* When colleagues work together as part of their professional learning experience, the tenor and nature of these interactions begin to alter the setting's overall professional culture toward one that is more collaborative. In this scenario, the benefits for participating educators "spill over," resulting in a workplace where educators are more likely to have each other's backs and to take collective responsibility for making and sustaining shifts in practice.

All too often, however, educators' professional learning opportunities are not sufficiently collaborative or interactive, similar to Jada's and Maria's experiences described in the chapter opening. While we do not know how much collaboration and interaction happened during their trainings, we do know that co-teachers Jada and Maria did not attend these trainings together, nor did they have formal opportunities to share what they learned with one another and others at their Center. Similarly, while all of the teachers were asked to view the same webinar, this viewing was not followed up with any formal collaborative opportunities to debrief and discuss.

Ultimately, it is only through collaboration and interaction that the link between professional learning and daily practice will be tightened. It is through collaborative experiences that educators can connect theory and rationale with tangible classroom strategies or activities, gaining the support they need to facilitate and scaffold these classroom applications. As illustrated in Figure 6.8, linking new learning to everyday practice should be framed by a cycle such that a classroom strategy is discussed and planned among educators. Then, for example, once that strategy is implemented in the classroom, at the next session, educators reflect on their experiences implementing the strategy and plan for refined implementation. We encourage leaders to use the checklist provided in Figure 6.9 to support the design of professional learning that effectively links new learning to everyday practice through educator collaboration.

Given the benefits of an approach to adult learning that fosters collaboration and interaction, how can we be sure we are incorporating learning opportunities that do just that? We encourage leaders to use the checklist provided in Figure 6.10 to guide site-level planning.

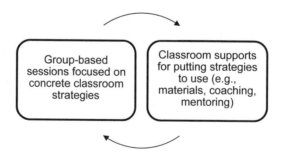

FIGURE 6.8. Tandem strategies for linking new learning to everyday practice.

Supports are in place for educators as they apply new ideas to everyday practice. This means . . .

Group-based sessions

☐ Integrate theory and rationale with practice-based activities (e.g., case studies, data analyses, demonstrations, lesson designs).

Classroom supports

☐ Materials necessary for implementing new knowledge are available and accessible.

☐ Nonevaluative observations and feedback are part of the ongoing routine.

☐ Schedules and classroom locations are organized to best encourage informal discussions about instruction.

FIGURE 6.9. Checklist for designing learning–practice links.

Collaboration and **interaction** are at the core of all sessions. At each session . . .

☐ Educators openly share thoughts, discuss perspectives, and raise questions (even when the question may reflect a lack of understanding).

☐ The environment is active, engaging educators in intellectually stimulating and practical dialogue.

☐ Participants reflect on the ideas with colleagues and give feedback.

FIGURE 6.10. Checklist for designing collaborative and interactive professional development.

Bringing It All Together:
Leading for Effective Professional Development

As we have said previously, it is an exciting time to be a leader in early educa-tion. The field is already experiencing a dramatic shift in the number of chil-dren accessing early education, and now is the time to embrace the opportu-nity to improve the quality of learning experiences across these settings. That change begins here, by transforming the format, substance, and structure of professional development to fully reflect the 21st-century model of adult learn-ing. By making professional learning opportunities intensive, by basing them on patterns in site-level data and practice, and by implementing them in a col-laborative and interactive way, early education leaders can support enhanced capacity among today's educators. But how does the leader implement this model in everyday practice? And how do we take into account the early educa-tor cornerstone competencies discussed in Part I of this book? Today's land-scape of early education professional development features two prominent and promising structures: PLCs and CCs. When implemented effectively, these structures bring these strategies to life.

In our own research and collaboration with early educators, we used these two structures to support and enhance the cornerstone competencies described in Part I of this book (i.e., executive functions, emotion regulation, relational skills, and talk for learning strategies). In the next three chapters, we spotlight these structures—their purpose, design, and key characteristics— and provide examples from our field experience that feature their effective use. Before reading on, however, be sure to utilize the many self-study tools embed-ded in this chapter to guide your thinking and planning around 21st-century adult learning.

Next, in Chapter 7 we discuss the content and design of effective learn-ing communities. We build upon the strategies for effective adult learning by exploring how they map to PLCs; we also discuss our work in developing early educators' cornerstone competencies through the PLC structure.

Effective Learning in Groups
Professional Learning Communities

Melinda glances at the clock. Twelve minutes have passed since the meeting's expected start time, but the group is still waiting for Maria, a PreK teacher. "Jada," Maria asks, "do you know why Maria isn't here yet?"

Jada shrugs. "I'm not sure. Maybe she forgot because we had to cancel our meeting last week?" Melinda decides to begin because teachers from all the other PreK classrooms are present. Their last meeting had to be cancelled owing to a conflict, so Melinda wants to use this time as efficiently as possible. "The purpose of our meeting today is to reflect on how the talk for learning strategy is working in your classrooms. The last time we met, I guess that was 3 weeks ago, we identified what has been going well for each of you. Today, let's start by sharing some of the challenges you're still experiencing with bringing more academic talk and conversations into your daily practice." The teachers sit silently. Melinda glances around the table and decides to pause and provide some wait time. "Anyone have a challenge they want to share or something that still feels hard?"

No one offers a response. One teacher scrolls through the smartphone in her lap. Another teacher glances around nervously, clearly uncomfortable. Melinda picks up on the energy level, and a cluster of questions begin to cloud her brain: "Do they think I'm trying to evaluate them?", "Is this uncomfortable because I'm the director?", "Doesn't she know it's rude to be on her phone during a meeting?", "Why isn't Maria here?" Just then, Maria rushes in. "I'm sorry I'm so late," she whispers breathlessly. "I didn't have coverage and Mario got picked up late. I couldn't leave him alone."

Like many of her colleagues, Melinda is experiencing a struggle that many early education leaders, directors, and coaches face: a meeting of professionals that feels inefficient, one-sided, and, simply put, not at all what was planned. So often, the professional meetings educators participate in outside of their direct work with children have unexpected variables; some feel rushed, others are unproductive, and still others feel unplanned or even overwhelming. Yet, ultimately, whether early education can deliver on its promise and potential depends, to a great degree, on whether the adults in the system can learn together—whether they can continually collaborate and improve in the service of high-quality early learning.

If we take adult learning seriously as a key lever in the effort to attain high-quality early learning environments, we have to confront a significant problem: We have not really prioritized adult learning in the way we have prioritized early learning in today's early education system. We have tasked adults in early education with the job of leading, designing, implementing, and sustaining daily learning environments characterized by challenging, nurturing interactions and learning opportunities. Importantly, at every level of the system, achieving those high-quality environments necessarily means planning and collaboration with other adults. One of the most powerful practices for implementing adult learning is to organize for learning in groups.

Organizing for genuine learning in groups means revisiting and reimagining the ways in which adults work and collaborate—whether in staff meetings, professional learning communities, or during more typical professional development trainings. Any time that is dedicated to the collective work and to adults being around a table learning together is one of the most precious resources in the system. And yet in many centers and conference rooms, there are missed opportunities—even time wasted—in getting to meaningful learning and improvement. There is never enough time, but rarely is the best use made of the time that adults *do* have together.

The problem of effective group learning, or lack thereof, demands a shift in thinking—one in which leaders work from the premise that every formal gathering of adults is potentially a rich opportunity for learning and building toward an even stronger learning community. Just as is the case with the early learning environment, gatherings designed for and/or with the potential for effective learning in groups (whether they are called staff meetings, professional learning communities, or teams), call for participants to be actively engaged in challenging tasks, grappling with problems, advancing their knowledge, and communicating with each other (Boudett & City, 2014). And just like the teacher in the early learning environment, the facilitator of group learning is focused on leveraging the different perspectives and learner profiles in the group—and, in turn, designing opportunities for all to deepen their knowledge through active engagement. In both settings, participants know the norms for behavior they are expected to follow. The design of the learning environment and learning activities reinforces these norms. (Boudett & City, 2014).

In this chapter, we discuss effective adult learning in groups. As we discussed in Chapter 6, there are a number of components that are vital to meaningful professional learning—learning that will change practice. And learning in groups is a key component in the movement toward building educator capacity and providing optimal learning environments for children. Here we emphasize design and implementation to ensure that, more often than not, groups that meet regularly make progress toward a shared mission of high-quality early learning for young children. While there are many different structures and names for learning in groups—staff meetings, monthly check-ins, study groups, periodic trainings—throughout the chapter, we use the professional learning community (PLC) as the case example. In what follows, in the context of our focus on learning in groups, we describe how a fruitful PLC can be achieved in the early education setting. We spotlight this professional learning structure and how it can be put to use in the early childhood educational setting. We delve into four key strategies for designing an effective PLC and provide examples of what these strategies looked like in our own work. We conclude by providing early education leaders with a self-study tool for considering the effectiveness of PLCs at the setting level.

Designing and Implementing Effective Learning in Groups: Professional Learning Communities as a Case Example

Elaborating on the traditional notion of a "meeting," establishing PLCs is one promising—and now quite popular—structure for getting to the capacity building that is needed to improve practice. PLCs are small, collaborative teams of educators and instructional leaders who meet regularly, working toward a plan for strengthening their practice. While the research base for this professional development strategy in education is only just beginning to accumulate—and the vast majority of that research is conducted in K–12 settings—evidence suggests that participating in PLCs improves educators' practices, supports collaborative professional cultures, and ultimately promotes children's learning (Bryk, Camburn, & Louis, 1999; Supovitz, 2002; Vescio, Ross, & Adams, 2008). In our own research and partnerships with early education settings, we implemented PLCs as a mechanism for bringing 21st-century adult-learning strategies to life (see Chapter 6). The results of our collaborations were promising and encouraging. As one participating educator told us, " [With traditional] training, you learn so much in one day, and then you forget it. Here [in PLCs], we learn something every day and then try it out in the classroom." And, it's not just that participating educators *felt* like PLC sessions were useful. In fact, they *were* useful. When we tested children's early literacy, vocabulary, and social–emotional skills, we saw the effects of this approach to professional and adult learning on their own early learning and development.

Professional Learning Communities: What They Are and What They Are Not

The field is now learning that, when PLCs are implemented effectively, they support educator learning and practice, while simultaneously benefitting the educational setting's culture. But before we examine the research-based strategies that proved to be effective for cultivating positive and productive PLC processes, we first outline the nuts and bolts of PLCs that form the foundation for those processes.

In particular, we would be remiss if we did not explicitly explain what PLCs are and what they are not. After all, education reform efforts, from early childhood through postsecondary education, too often "drift" from the intended design of a particular reform strategy such that, in the end, the reform looks quite similar to traditional practices, only under a new name. Moreover, as PLCs begin to take hold, it's worth remembering that any given group of educators engaging in some form of professional learning does not necessarily comprise a PLC. For instance, we would definitely think twice before calling Melinda's meeting at the opening of the chapter a PLC. Before we become too casual with the term and it begins to lose meaning, it is important to identify formats and strategies that are *not* characteristic of PLCs. In Figure 7.1, we share a list of approaches to training and development that may have

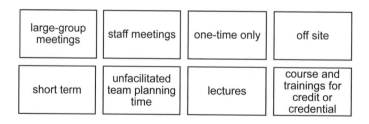

FIGURE 7.1. PLCs: What they are not.

their place in the professional lives of educators, but certainly do not qualify as legitimate PLCs.

Key Features of PLCs

Well, if Figure 7.1 shows us what PLCs are not, then what are the characteristics of an authentic and effective PLC? In what follows, we outline four critical features.

A PLC Is a Small, Collaborative Group of Educators

A PLC includes a small group of educators working together in the same school or center or in partner centers and schools that regularly collaborate (e.g., a feeder early education center and the local public school, a home-care setting and a neighboring multiclassroom center). This group of educators typically consists of co-teaching teams—the teachers, assistant teachers, and/or paraprofessionals who work together in the same classrooms. Members might also include the specialists or coaches who work with participating educators and the children in their care.

A PLC Has a Skilled Facilitator

A PLC by definition includes a skilled facilitator who can guide the instruction and dialogue, steering the group along its planned path. This facilitator might be a coach, specialist, or teacher leader. Ideally, she will also serve as a classroom coach (see Chapter 8). This facilitator is most effective if she is skilled in recognizing and applying best practices in the early education field, often gained through experience, continuous learning, and reflection; but also key to this role is the ability to *mentor adults*. A skilled facilitator might have one foot in the field, living these experiences side by side with teachers, assistants, and paraprofessionals, while also demonstrating an ability to understand and direct adults, guide them in their professional learning, and ideally possess a grounded vision for growth or change.

In our experience with PLCs, supervisors did not serve as facilitators, nor were they members of the PLC. Why not include supervisors? Well, particularly when focusing on cornerstone educator competencies (see Part I), PLC sessions involve candid conversations and critical self-reflection; we found that evaluations (real and perceived) should not be a part of these sessions. Recall Melinda's struggle to elicit responses from the teachers about challenges. These teachers were likely unresponsive, and perhaps even a bit nervous to divulge any challenges, because they felt they might be evaluated. It is certainly difficult for an educator to admit to an area of struggle if there is the potential to be judged; our experience taught us that it was more productive for someone other than the director or administrator to take the role of a PLC facilitator to avoid emotional complexity and also to increase honest communication. In Melinda's case, she might consider appointing someone else as the facilitator.

A PLC Is Held On Site

PLC sessions are easily accessible and are typically held in a center or school setting. Educators assemble at their center or school in a consistent and appropriate space (away from children). To avoid the struggle Maria experienced in the chapter's opening, a PLC meeting should be easily accessible physically to all educators involved, with coverage issues and time constraints considered ahead of time.

A PLC Meets Consistently

PLC meetings are both *regular* and *frequent*—for example, on an hour-long, weekly basis. And these regular, frequent meetings are *ongoing*: These groups convene consistently throughout the school year, and optimally, they continue to meet for many years (see Chapter 6 on the importance of designing *intensive* professional development opportunities that are frequent, ongoing, and cohesive). At the Explorations Early Learning Center, the PLC meetings had become infrequent. The far better scenario calls for PLCs to be prioritized, such that the work from each meeting can consistently advance toward a specified goal.

Early education leaders need to ensure that the PLCs at their sites are designed to include these features, so that they will run smoothly and effectively. Consider Melinda and the challenges she encountered because key PLC components were missing. When launching a PLC in your setting or evaluating the design of your existing PLC strategy, use the self-study checklist in Figure 7.2 to guide your thinking.

What Are the Strategies Required for Designing Effective Professional Learning Communities?

Convening a small group of co-teaching teams at a site regularly and frequently may not result in professional growth that translates into enhanced learning environments for children. Getting the right nuts and bolts in place to set the

☐   We have a skilled facilitator present.

☐   Co-teaching teams are participating.

☐   Specialists or other educators that work with participating teachers are present.

☐   Group sessions are onsite in a consistent and appropriate space
     (away from children).

☐   Sessions occur frequently (for example, weekly or twice a month).

☐   Ongoing (in it for the long haul!)

☐   PLCs are regular (predictable part of educators' schedules).

FIGURE 7.2. A nuts-and-bolts checklist for designing PLCs.

stage for cultivating a PLC is only the first step. To genuinely support professional growth, the next important task is designing an approach and learning plan that the community will engage in. As we learned in Chapter 6, for professional development to be most effective, the plan should be grounded in data-driven, site-level needs, and the approach should be both collaborative and embedded in practice. In the context of a PLC, how do we put these principles of effective professional development into practice? In the sections that follow, and as illustrated in Figure 7.3, we outline four design strategies that should guide the work of PLCs.

Leading effective PLCs means:

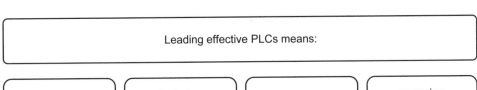

| using a goal-driven scope and sequence that builds incrementally | fostering collaboration and supportive relationships among participants | anchoring learning in concrete connections to daily practice | engaging participants as decision makers and co-constructors of strategies |

FIGURE 7.3. Key strategies for designing effective PLCs.

Strategy 1: Use a Goal-Driven Scope and Sequence That Builds Incrementally

If the work of PLCs is to result in enhanced educator practice, it must reside within a larger plan for learning (Supovitz, 2002). Recall from Chapter 6 that early education leaders can use already existing data to pinpoint patterns in site-level needs and then zero in on a limited number of professional learning goals. These relevant and high-impact goals drive the scope of the work to be accomplished in the PLC, ensuring focused and targeted PLC sessions that, over time, can accomplish deep learning.

| using a goal-driven scope and sequence that builds incrementally |
| fostering collaboration and supportive relationships among participants |
| anchoring learning in concrete connections to daily practice |
| engaging participants as decision makers and co-constructors of strategies |

We can use this scope to design more specific objectives that build incrementally from one to the next, toward our ultimate goal(s). What do we mean by build incrementally? As opposed to creating a learning plan that presents a laundry list of stand-alone objectives, we organize the learning plan in a way that very intentionally links the sequencing of objectives to the ways in which the target competencies develop. Each objective, then, connects to the next one, and focusing on the former supports work on the latter. In this way, educators are continually "stretching" their knowledge by digging deeper into what they know and do. Session by session, incremental, genuine, and sustained transformations in practices can occur.

When we use PLC sessions to construct and enhance knowledge incrementally, educators can accomplish many important tasks—grapple with ideas, analyze current practices, reconcile inconsistencies, arrive at conclusions, and refine and extend expertise. We are not just layering new teaching strategies on top of entrenched difficulties that will continue to affect classroom interactions and learning (think of a Band-Aid approach), but instead, we are slowly and intentionally developing competencies that address root causes.

What Might This Look Like?

In our own work with early educators, we designed a scope and sequence that focused on building the cornerstone educator competencies that were described in Part I and are summarized in Figure 7.4 (introduced in Chapter 1 as Figure 1.3). We focused on these competencies because they are fundamental to carrying out and effectively managing the daily physical, emotional, and mental labor that providing high-quality early education demands. But enhancing these competencies among early educators cannot be accomplished

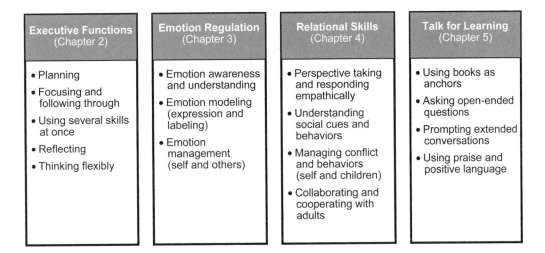

FIGURE 7.4. Recap: Cornerstone educator competencies.

in a stepwise manner by simply checking one, and then the next, off the list. Instead, we had to design a scope and sequence that reflects what we know about how these competencies are cultivated and refined among adult learners.

Specifically, Figure 7.5 provides a bird's-eye view of how we think about sequencing objectives to match the incremental process of enhancing these cornerstone competencies. As you can see, we designed four broad modules (or units) around four related topics:

1. Creating a reflective professional community.
2. Analyzing classroom stress: When, where, and why?
3. Applying strategies for nurturing ourselves and others.
4. Enhancing relationships in the service of teaching and learning.

And when we say that these topics were addressed through an incremental process, *we mean it!* These four modules spanned the school year. The following year, we worked on further refining these same competencies, focusing on the implementation of strategies learned and practiced the year before.

How do these modules follow a sequence that matches the ways in which cornerstone competencies develop? Let's consider Module 1. In this first module, we take significant time to focus on the professional learning community itself—co-constructing norms, generating collective goals, inspiring agency, and ensuring a shared understanding of best practices. We start with a concentration on community building because cornerstone competencies are close to the bone: Focusing on emotions and relationships can bring vulnerabilities to

Module 1. Creating a reflective professional community

Build community norms (relationship skills).

Understand the instrumental role of early educators in children's development.

Co-construct goals for the group (executive functioning).

Identify individual goals (executive functions).

Understand foundational classroom practices (talk for learning).

Plan lessons that use books as anchors for learning and extended conversations (executive functions; talk for learning).

Observe and document classroom stress (emotion regulation).

Module 2. Analyzing classroom stress: When, where, and why?

Use observation, documentation, and reflection to identify classroom stressors, monitor responses, and determine triggers (emotion regulation).

Plan lessons focused on labeling and discussing emotions in the classroom (talk for learning; executive functions).

Reflect on emotional learning in the classroom (emotion regulation; executive functions).

Module 3. Applying strategies for nurturing ourselves

Use emotion management strategies to address physical signs of negative stress and the thoughts and perceptions fueling that stress (emotion regulation).

Design and consistently use routines that address patterns in classroom stress (executive functions; talk for learning).

Use praise, positive language, and engaging classroom conversations as classroom management and teaching strategies (talk for learning).

Module 4. Enhancing

Identify the perspectives of others (relationship skills).

Manage conflict using empathic, respectful, and assertive communication (relationship skills).

Design and consistently use routines that promote positive classroom relationships (relationship skills; talk for learning; executive functions).

Mentor others to support cohesive instructional approaches across the setting (relationship skills).

FIGURE 7.5. Example incremental sequence for building cornerstone educator competencies.

the surface, and reflecting critically and collaboratively on teaching practices has the potential to uncover weaknesses. As such, for this important work to move forward, a cohesive and trusting community with shared knowledge is foundational.

Taking another example of a work sequence that reflects how cornerstone competencies develop, notice how emotion regulation skills and relationship skills are organized. Emotion regulation skills are more heavily addressed in the first three modules, while relationship skills—although they absolutely play a role early on—become an even stronger area of focus in the final module. This decision represents the importance of cultivating self-awareness and self-regulation as prerequisites for strengthening relationships.

Importantly, another feature of the cornerstone competencies is that they are never fully mastered; they are "growth competencies" that can, and should, be cultivated and refined throughout an educator's career. Therefore, note that objectives in this scope and sequence are never relinquished (represented by the arrows in Figure 7.5). We continue to extend and reinforce previous goals through purposeful repetition as we work on new, but related, ones. As such, educators continually have the opportunity to add to the complex competencies addressed in prior sessions.

Stay the Course
When Everything Else Feels Much More Pressing . . .

When convening a small group of educators working together in the same school or center, there is never a shortage of issues to discuss. From how to handle the child who started biting his peers, to what to do about the family that is continuously late for pick up, to the latest changes in regulations and standards—fodder for conversation abounds! So the question is: When do we pause and use PLC time toward immediately pressing issues, and when do we put the latest "crisis" aside and stay the course?

As a rule of thumb, we do not use PLC sessions for day-to-day problem solving without also connecting this problem solving to the PLC objectives (e.g., reflecting on emotional responses, trying to understand varying perspectives). In the best of cases, these pressing issues demonstrate important teachable moments that we can take advantage of in meeting our goals. But—unless the physical or emotional well-being of a student or educator is at stake—discussions revolving around the latest issue or dilemma should not displace or detract from this important time focused on bigger-picture challenges and root causes.

Strategy 2: Foster Collaboration and Supportive Relationships among Participants

As you might recall from Chapter 6, collaborative and interactive learning experiences are key to enhancing educator practices. Learning, by its very nature, is social. When professional development provides ongoing opportunities to talk ideas through and grapple with them together, rather than just reading or listening to learn, knowledge is deepened and misunderstandings are clarified.

using a goal-driven scope and sequence that builds incrementally

fostering collaboration and supportive relationships among participants

anchoring learning in concrete connections to daily practice

engaging participants as decision makers and co-constructors of strategies

Because PLCs in particular meet regularly and frequently and are made up of educator teams that work together in the same center or school, the effect of collaborative and interactive learning experiences is not limited to individual educator's knowledge development. Instead, collaborative PLC activities and tasks, in and of themselves, are a platform for strengthening relationships among participants (Goddard, Goddard, & Tschannen-Moran, 2007). And strong relationships among educators matter! Collaborative and supportive relationships among the adults in an education setting are the soil in which healthy learning climates and strong instruction grow (see Chapter 4). PLCs provide a testing ground for engaging in the kinds of positive interactions it takes to build collaborative and supportive professional relationships.

What Might This Look Like?

In our own partnerships with early educators, we facilitated PLCs that worked toward the scope and sequence presented in Figure 7.5. During this work, whether the specific objective being considered was relationship based (e.g., identify the perspectives of others) or not (e.g., plan lessons that use books as anchors for learning), reinforcing supportive and collaborative relationships among participants was central. How did we accomplish this? Every PLC session involved interactive discussions and team-based work. What's more, we intentionally scaffolded this collaboration and periodically reflected as a whole group on the collaboration process itself.

Let's take an example to shed light on what we mean. As you might notice in Figure 7.5, instructional planning is a consistent feature from module to module. In our work, "instructional planning" almost always meant "coplanning" with other educators. To support both the act of instructional planning and collaborative relationships, the PLC facilitator circulated from group to group in order to ensure that all voices were heard, modeling perspective taking and facilitating compromise. Once teaching teams had co-developed instructional plans to further encourage supportive relationships among educators in the PLC, each team shared its plans and concerns. Other PLC members then provided feedback and problem solved with the presenters. Often, when sharing plans, other teaching teams revised their own instructional plans in order to integrate the good ideas of their colleagues. Over time, this small- and whole-group collaboration helped to cultivate a supportive professional culture within PLC sessions—a culture that seeped into daily interactions outside of the sessions.

Strategy 3: Anchor Learning in Concrete Connections to Daily Practice

The focus of PLCs is often an abstract, perhaps discrete, strategy or topic. For example, enhancing executive functioning or emotion regulation in the classroom does not conjure up immediately obvious strategies for the educator. Even explicit instructional goals, such as using classroom talk to bolster children's learning, can be complex and challenging to initially wrap our heads around

> using a goal-driven scope and sequence that builds incrementally

> fostering collaboration and supportive relationships among participants

> anchoring learning in concrete connections to daily practice

> engaging participants as decision makers and co-constructors of strategies

owing to a likely gap between educational theory and practice. To be sure, this does not mean that we stray from enhancing educator competencies that are "hard to explain." If the work of PLCs is to result in professional growth, we absolutely want to emphasize the competencies that underlie effective teaching (rather than exclusively focusing on discrete or technical teaching strategies), but it would also be unwise to always work in the theoretical mode without grounding the conversation in tangible classroom strategies and examples. In this vein, when working on abstract competencies, we might start with a task or example from daily practice that shines a light on something familiar, and then, after several PLC sessions, connect these concrete classroom tasks or examples to the conceptually less familiar and less tangible competencies.

What Might This Look Like?

To illustrate what we mean, let's take an example. In Module 2 of the scope and sequence presented in Figure 7.5, educators use observation, documentation, and reflection to identify classroom stressors, to monitor responses, and to determine triggers. Ultimately, a key understanding that emerges from this work is the reciprocal nature of interactions: the notion that educators' actions trigger emotions and behaviors in their students, which, in turn, prompt subsequent responses in educators (see Chapter 2). This cycle makes sense on the surface, though it is sometimes hard for early educators to "see" it in their own classroom interactions. Until early educators understand the ways in which this cycle plays out in their own contexts, they cannot alter their own responses for the purpose of attaining a regulated learning environment. For example, in Module 3, it would be difficult to design routines that address patterns in classroom stress if we do not first recognize and identify those patterns. (Perhaps, in more traditional professional development, designing and implementing classroom routines would be the starting place, but in this approach, we prioritize educator competencies and teaching processes above discrete strategies.)

So how did we support educators to understand and respond to the reciprocal nature of interactions? We started by concretizing emotional responses using a documentation task, in which educators noted emotional responses during difficult times of day by jotting down information on a Post-it a few times a week. Then, during PLC sessions, we used these documented, concrete examples to begin to engage in relatively sophisticated and abstract analyses of

What Concrete Connections to Classroom Practice Means for Educator Buy-In

Anchoring learning in concrete connections to the classroom supports educators' knowledge development and practices—but that's not all. This PLC strategy is also important for buy-in, especially early on. For many educators, understandably, there is a desire to have something to "try tomorrow." This desire (or expectation) runs counter to the focus of early PLC sessions (i.e., community building, goal development, and beginning to understand current practices). Therefore, we strongly recommend integrating concrete classroom strategies into the work of PLCs right from the start.

For example, notice that in the scope and sequence we used (Figure 7.5), an objective of Module 1 is using books as anchors for learning. To be sure, this objective fits with our overall goals for the PLC—this talk for learning strategy is paramount in the early childhood classroom, and planning for joint book reading is a useful way to apply executive functioning skills. But focusing on this objective from the start also meant that educators immediately received high-quality children's literature for their classrooms and were able to plan strong lessons around them. Educators' responses to our early work using children's literature was exceedingly positive; the instructional planning and reflection, made possible by acquiring this literature, stimulated rich PLC conversations, even as we were spending significant time working primarily toward building a reflective and collaborative professional community.

what was transpiring during difficult moments. We consistently asked reflective prompts (e.g., "What tends to happen when you react in a particular way?"), and charted how educators and children were acting and feeling during these moments. In addition, we read and analyzed brief case examples featuring relevant classroom experiences, concentrating on how the showcased educators and children were influencing one another's responses. Ultimately, after analyzing educators' lived experiences in combination with brief and relevant case examples, we developed strategies educators can use to help manage stress in the classroom (see Chapters 2, 3, and 4)—ones that emphasize the reciprocal nature of interactions. Once this thorough understanding was developed, we returned to the theoretical realm to design strategies for improving interactions, and we further analyzed classroom relationships.

Strategy 4: Engage Participants as Decision Makers and Co-Constructors of Strategies

Effective PLCs engage in practices that reflect both (1) the high value placed on community members' knowledge and lived experiences and (2) the importance of participants' active involvement in knowledge creation for their learning, engagement, and sustained uptake of new practices (Lieberman & Miller, 2011; Vescio et al., 2008). As such, during PLC sessions, the facilitator consistently and strategically releases responsibility to participants, enabling them to take a leadership role in designing and customizing the learning experience. Importantly, when we engage PLC members as decision makers and co-constructors, we are not straying from or rerouting our thoughtfully designed goals and plans based on group members' opinions or judgments. On the contrary, this strategy, when implemented effectively, increases the efficacy of our work rather than substantively changing it. In practical terms, this strategy ensures that PLC members regularly have opportunities to

> using a goal-driven scope and sequence that builds incrementally

> fostering collaboration and supportive relationships among participants

> anchoring learning in concrete connections to daily practice

> engaging participants as decision makers and co-constructors of strategies

- decide on group processes,
- tailor classroom strategies to their needs and their students' needs, and
- facilitate discussions and collaborative work.

Ultimately, participating educators become the agents of their own learning and the learning process, and, as a result, the improvements realized from PLCs are poised for sustainability.

What Might This Look Like?

Engaging participants as decision makers and co-constructors of strategies was instrumental to our facilitation of PLCs in early education settings. This strategy permeated all facets of our work and was continually linked to participant engagement, investment, and uptake. Table 7.1 presents real-life examples of how this particular PLC strategy was put to use.

Bringing It All Together: Leading Learning Settings with Effective Professional Learning Communities

As we have learned, the professional learning community is a natural place to develop educator capacity, surrounded by collaborative colleagues with a shared experience. PLCs offer a professional development structure that is consistent and intensive, that encourages collaboration and reflection, and that relates directly to practice with students.

How can early education leaders ensure that PLCs meet these goals? Using PLCs as a tool can certainly support quality improvement at their sites, as long as leaders understand that the PLC is a platform or structure—and that ultimately the content and process embedded within the PLC structure will makes the difference. Leaders also need to remember that building effective PLC communities takes time and forethought; planning and crafting a scope and sequence around a specific goal and knowing how to execute a plan to achieve the goal is integral to getting on the right track early (see Chapter 9). And after leaders have PLCs up and running, there is a need to be mindful that cultivating relationships of trust and collaboration and a culture of shared learning also takes time.

Once leaders have an understanding of the components of an effective PLC, we encourage them to consider their own experiences with PLCs. Figure 7.6 is designed to support leaders as they consider professional learning in their setting—it embodies a co-constructed philosophy of how PLCs can promote effective change. In our work, we found this image as foundational both to our vision and to our success as a working PLC group. We also encourage leaders to use the self-study tool in Figure 7.7 to guide their next steps in establishing a new PLC, adapting some features of what currently resembles a PLC at their site(s) if applicable, or nudging an already existing PLC in a more effective direction.

Next, in Chapter 8, we explore how coaching, integrated with the PLC model, adds another important structural layer to establishing effective professional learning. We refer to this model as connected coaching, unpack its elements, and provide strategies for establishing and implementing a connected coaching model.

TABLE 7.1. Sample Opportunities for Engaging Educators as Leaders, Decision Makers, and Co-Constructors

PLC processes: Designing and using group discussion norms (Chapter 4)

Group norms are co-developed by community members. The group regularly reflects on the ways in which, collectively, the norms are observed, noting how the group might improve, and brainstorming ways that the norms could be revised to better reflect current group needs and values.

PLC processes: Using instructional reflection protocols (Chapter 2)

PLC members take turns using the reflection protocol to lead these group conversations. When taking on this leadership role, the PLC member poses questions and prompts further reflection, offers insights and suggestions, and attends to group norms.

PLC goals: Setting (Chapter 2)

When launching the PLC, the facilitator shares the diagram that represents the PLC's goals and how these goals will be met (see Figure 7.6). Then, participants critically analyze this diagram and present suggestions for improvements. For example, the language used to describe goals or the work might be revised to better reflect educators' experiences. Participants might also have ideas for how the change process will occur, offering suggestions for how the diagram itself might be revised to better reflect what the PLC will accomplish. This co-constructed visual becomes a touchstone for the ongoing work.

Strategies: Designing a visual scale for rating emotional responses (Chapter 3)

The facilitator introduces a visual scale that can be used for rating stress. To start, the visual includes a scale, for example, from 0 to 5, for describing levels of stress, but no descriptions of what these different stress levels feel like. The group collaboratively generates these descriptions, adding them to the graphic tool (see Chapter 3 for a full description of this strategy). Now, using the language generated by the group, the visual scale is ready to be used as a shared tool for rating and describing stressful experiences, and, as a result, for encouraging emotional awareness.

Strategies: Designing classroom routines that promote relationships (Chapters 4 and 5)

The facilitator explains guiding principles for routines that promote positive classroom relationships and shares examples of routines that apply these principles. PLC members then decide how their current classroom routines should be revised in accordance with these principles, or whether they need to launch a new routine that applies them. For example, the facilitator might explain the importance of prompting back-and-forth conversations among children and provide the "Think–Pair–Share" routine as an example classroom routine that supports conversations, but then educators might tailor this routine, or create a different one, that accomplishes the same goal but best fits their particular classroom context.

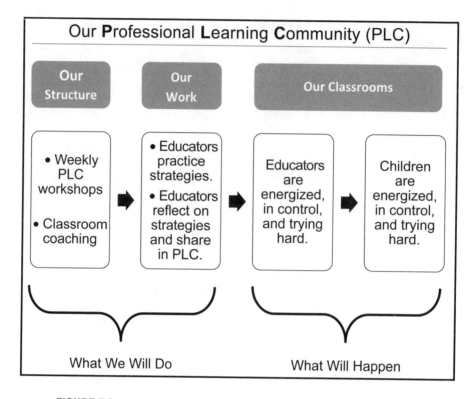

FIGURE 7.6. Example of co-constructed theory of change for PLCs.

Leaders can design and implement PLCs by . . .	What do you notice about your existing PLCs?	What overall patterns or trends do you notice?
using a goal-driven scope and sequence that builds incrementally.		
fostering collaboration and supportive relationships.		
anchoring learning in concrete connections to daily practice.		
engaging participants as decision makers and co-constructors of knowledge.		

FIGURE 7.7. Self-study tool for PLCs.

CHAPTER 8

Connected Coaching

Jada glances around her PreK room at the Explorations Early Learning Center with a freshly critical eye. Ever since Melinda, the center's director, brought Karen, the new coach, on to the center's staff, Jada has become a little more aware of her classroom organization—and her teaching, for that matter. Jada wonders what today's meeting will be like; they are scheduled to debrief a lesson Jada taught a few days ago. Jada isn't sure what she thinks of all this. But she smiles, remembering her pleasant surprise when Karen stayed around after the lesson, helping to wipe down tables and get the children ready for lunch. It was like she understood.

As Karen enters the room, ready for the meeting with her notebook and two cold waters from the break room, she says: "Alright, we have work to do together. I'm looking forward to this!" Karen smiles. She looks Jada in the eye. "Does it work for you to start now? Let's sit down and get started—I want to talk about some great things I noticed at circle time yesterday morning, and I'd love to hear more about what you thought." Jada smiles tentatively, and they walk to the table and sit down. Karen hands Jada a bottle of water and gets out the protocol they will work from. Jada takes a sip and thinks, "Maybe this won't be so bad."

In this new and dynamic era of early education, when demands on early educators are significant and the expectations of early education as a strategy for boosting early learning and development are even greater, as we discussed in Chapter 6, research (and common sense) tells us that professional development is critical to improving classroom quality (Neuman & Cunningham, 2009; Sheridan, Edwards, Marvin, & Knoche, 2009).

Today, coaching is the approach to professional development that is perhaps most popular—there is a lot of momentum for coaching to be included as a key component of reform efforts, guided by the promise that it will result in improved teaching and learning (Zaslow et al., 2010, 2011). And research supports this momentum; many studies demonstrate that educators who receive coaching have a greater likelihood of engaging more deeply and effectively in the teaching practices they are learning than are educators receiving more traditional forms of professional development, such as courses (e.g., Neuman & Wright, 2010). And not only does coaching show a capacity for producing gains in the quality of teaching and learning, some research suggests it also may be a powerful tool for increasing educators' beliefs about their teaching ability and effectiveness—and therefore their confidence in trying out new practices (Tschannen-Moran & McMaster, 2009).

So in many ways, ongoing support and encouragement—in the form of coaching—are thought of as essential to professional learning opportunities. But what is coaching, exactly? Well, coaching is conceptualized as a strategy that aims to do a few things: cultivate educator knowledge of teaching and learning; offer modeling of effective instruction and then a chance for educators to engage in that targeted practice with support; and give educators an opportunity to receive constructive, supportive feedback and to engage in troubleshooting about effective implementation of the developing practice(s). In general, the coach typically models strategies in the classroom, performs targeted observations of classroom practices, and provides supportive feedback on these practices (Neuman & Cunningham, 2009).

In this chapter, we review a coaching model, called *connected coaching*, that pairs with the group learning we described in Chapter 7. Based on the research we have cited, next we outline this model's key elements and offer protocols to help early education leaders put effective coaching into action.

Coaching: What It Is and What It Is Not

As described, coaching is an individualized professional development strategy in which a coach supports educators as they apply the knowledge and strategies learned in group-training sessions to their classrooms. To do this important work, the coach regularly and frequently visits classrooms, simultaneously observing classroom processes and providing hands-on support. Then, following this visit, the educator and coach discuss the content of the visit and use this joint reflection to inform the next steps.

What makes the coaching model we're going to describe *connected*? Here, we are taking advantage of the multiple meanings of connection, referring to both (1) the links this model makes between group learning and classroom practice and (2) the key role that the coach–educator relationship plays in supporting professional growth and changes in practice. In what follows, we dig into both types of connection.

First, as illustrated in Figure 8.1, this approach to coaching provides a bridge (or two-way connection) between classrooms and group-training sessions. To establish this important connection, the classroom coach is often also the person who leads group-learning sessions. He or she then

- scaffolds and troubleshoots the classroom implementation of strategies discussed in group sessions, and
- uses the information gleaned from the coaching process to tailor group-learning sessions in ways that respond to patterns in group members' experiences.

Connected coaching can be linked to any number of group-learning models that embody the characteristics of effective professional learning we describe in Chapter 6. In our work, connected coaching supports educators as they implement the knowledge and strategies that are addressed in PLCs (see Chapter 7). In our approach, the same skilled facilitator who leads the site's PLC sessions also serves as the coach, and the coaching revolves around the same goal-driven scope and sequence that guides PLC work.

The second characteristic that makes this coaching model *connected* is the actual connection—the relationship—mindfully forged between the coach and the educator. To fully realize the promise of coaching to improve learning and teaching, coaches and educators must establish partnerships that are marked by trust, mutual respect, and open communication, and that are personalized

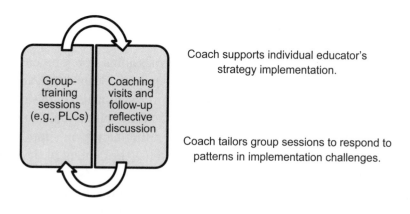

FIGURE 8.1. What makes coaching *connected*?

Recap of PLCs

PLCs are site-based, intensive professional development structures. They involve small, collaborative teams of educators and instructional leaders who meet frequently and regularly, working toward a long-term plan for strengthening their practices. These meetings are guided by a skilled facilitator who ensures that PLC sessions are

- guided by a goal-driven scope and sequence that builds incrementally,
- collaborative and focused on relationship building,
- anchored in concrete connections to daily practice,
- co-constructed with participants.

PLCs are key to supporting genuine professional learning among early educators, but translating the group learning that takes place during PLCs (outside of classrooms) into individual behavior change (inside the classroom) requires postgroup-session supports that facilitate and scaffold classroom applications. This is where connected coaching comes into play.

and flexible enough to meet the needs of diverse contexts, educators, and children. Why is this relationship foundational to connected coaching? Well, from the educator's perspective, having teaching observed and subjected to constructive feedback—and *then* trying new approaches to strengthen practice—is not easy. Therefore, a positive relationship between the educator and coach, one that unites evaluation and discussion with trust and respect, is crucial. Only once a foundation of trust is established can the educator–coach relationship be leveraged for the purpose of enhancing practice.

Voices from the Field
The Power of Coaching That's Connected

Content Connections

"The activities [learned during PLCs] were based on the classroom observations, not 'cookie cutter' activities . . . they were built around what was actually going on in the classroom."

Relational Connections

"It wasn't like the coach was there to crack the whip on you, or to observe you and make sure that you were doing everything right. She never gave that feeling. You felt like she was there to help better everything."

Before we delve into the research-based strategies that make connected coaching happen, we need to remind ourselves that any and all activities labeled as "coaching" may not qualify as such in the 21st-century professional learning sense of the word. As coaching continues to spread as a reform strategy in today's early education environment, in many settings not only is coaching poorly defined for coaches and educators and disconnected from many other professional development activities in the setting, but it also lacks many of the other necessary ingredients of effective professional learning. At worst, today's coaching efforts take an evaluative tone, and, at best, they are strong with respect to the coach–educator relationship, but they are not connected to a larger site-based strategy for educator development and instructional change. Thus, before we become too casual with the term connected coaching and allow it to lose meaning, we want to be very precise in our description of the format, focus, and general approach that make it effective. To that end, Figure 8.2 contrasts common coaching pitfalls with the core features of authentic connected coaching.

	Common Coaching Pitfalls	Connected Coaching
Format	• Classroom visits are sporadic, infrequent, or unreliable. • Classroom visits lack any follow-up, or too much time passes between visits and follow-up conversations.	• Classroom visits are ongoing, frequent, and planned. • Classroom visits are always tied to timely, reflective conversations.
Focus	• Coaching focuses on accreditation or licensing requirements (i.e., compliance monitoring).	• Coaching focuses on the same goal-driven scope and sequence that guides group-training sessions.
Approach	• The coach takes an evaluative, supervisory, or punitive stance. • The coach establishes a friendly relationship with the educator, but never moves past a "culture of nice." • Either the coach is hands-off (sitting in the back taking notes) or overly hands-on, such that classroom change resides in the coach, not in educator learning.	• The coach takes a nonjudgmental, supportive, and responsive stance. • A strong, mutually respectful coach–educator relationship is the means for having critical conversations about practice. • The coach is a hands-on observer who supports the educator's efforts, plans, and professional growth.

FIGURE 8.2. Connected coaching: What it is and what it is not.

What Strategies Make for Effective Connected Coaching?

In the sections that follow, we offer a selection of strategies for putting connected coaching into practice. We outline three principal design strategies that should guide the work of connected coaching, as illustrated in Figure 8.3. First, we describe the value of ongoing, frequent classroom visits that involve simultaneous observation and hands-on classroom participation. Next, we delve into the individualized, reflective discussions that follow these classroom visits. Throughout these sections describing specific coaching strategies, we highlight how the role of the educator–coach relationship is fostered and leveraged.

Strategy 1: Conduct Hands-On, Participatory Classroom Observations

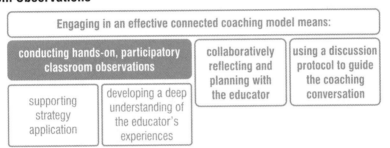

In this model of classroom support and on-the-job professional learning, the coach and educator schedule regular and frequent visits to the educator's classroom. In our own work, these hands-on, participatory classroom observations were fundamental to promoting the key educator competencies described in Part I. They were an essential component of our theory of improvement and

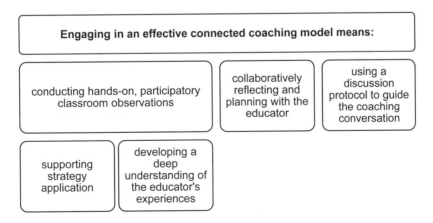

FIGURE 8.3. Key components of effective connected coaching models.

were cited by participants as instrumental for their own learning and growth. Figure 8.4 presents a play-by-play of the coach's steps and goals before, during, and immediately following the visit. Highlighted in the "During the Visit" section of Figure 8.4, these participatory classroom observations serve to accomplish two, interrelated goals:

1. Support educators' application of competencies and strategies discussed during group-learning sessions, and
2. Develop a deep understanding of educators' day-to-day experiences (in their particular professional contexts).

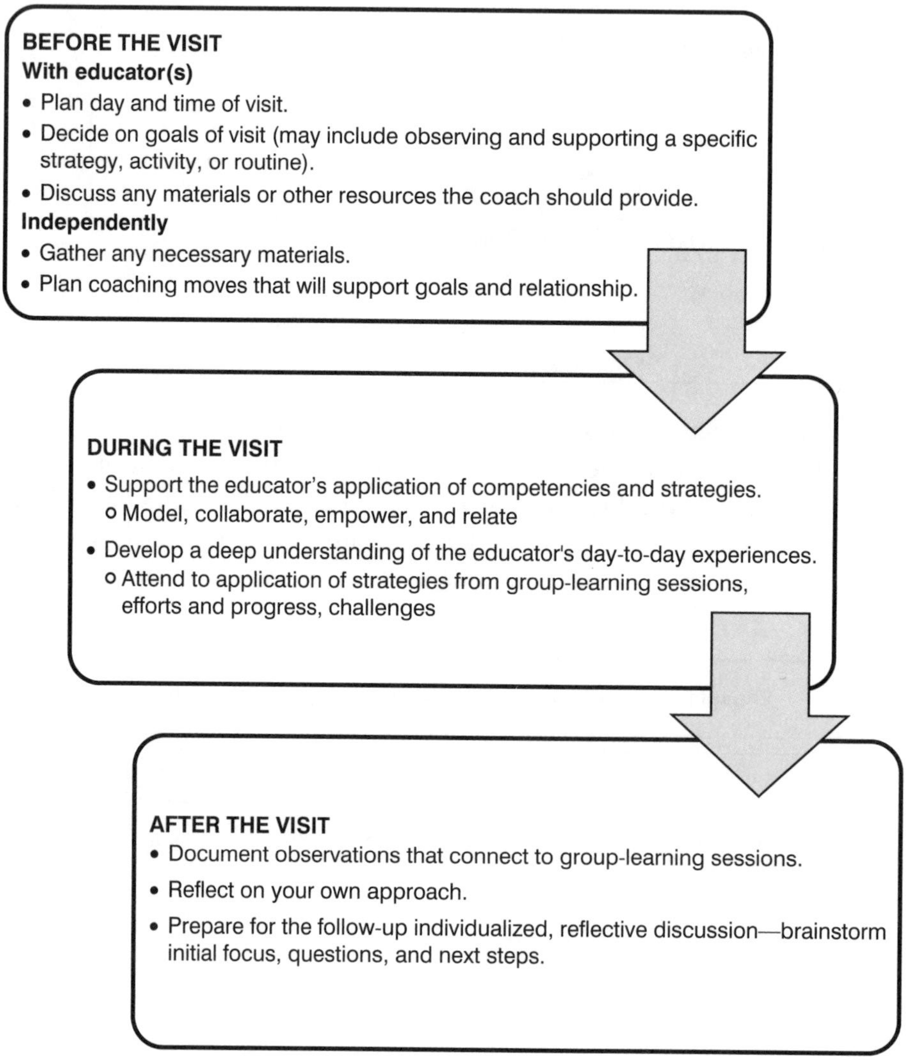

BEFORE THE VISIT
With educator(s)
• Plan day and time of visit.
• Decide on goals of visit (may include observing and supporting a specific strategy, activity, or routine).
• Discuss any materials or other resources the coach should provide.
Independently
• Gather any necessary materials.
• Plan coaching moves that will support goals and relationship.

DURING THE VISIT
• Support the educator's application of competencies and strategies.
  o Model, collaborate, empower, and relate
• Develop a deep understanding of the educator's day-to-day experiences.
  o Attend to application of strategies from group-learning sessions, efforts and progress, challenges

AFTER THE VISIT
• Document observations that connect to group-learning sessions.
• Reflect on your own approach.
• Prepare for the follow-up individualized, reflective discussion—brainstorm initial focus, questions, and next steps.

FIGURE 8.4. The participatory observation play-by-play.

Voices from the Field
Participatory Classroom Observations

"[It made such a difference] to see what they [the PLC facilitators] were teaching us, to be practiced by her [the coach] in the classroom. Like, okay, I may not have done it that way, but if it worked when she did it, okay, let me try it that way."

The sections that follow delve into how these tandem goals are accomplished.

Supporting Strategy Application

As we noted earlier, a core feature of connected coaching is that it scaffolds the application of strategies discussed during group professional learning sessions. So, in the educator's classroom, the coach intentionally and thoughtfully models target competencies, collaborates with the educator to help her act on specific strategies, empowers the educator to independently apply new knowledge, and consistently forges the coach–educator relationship. These coaching "moves" are detailed in Figure 8.5.

The coach accomplishes these goals by taking a *hands-on participatory approach*. Upon entering the classroom, the coach does not take a seat at the back to quietly scribble notes, nor does the coach take over instruction. Instead, the coach comes in as an engaged and active observer—one who interacts with the children and participates in the day's activities along with the class, supporting the educator's plans and routines along the way. And, as an added consequence, by rolling up her sleeves, taking part in children's and teachers' days, and expressing an understanding of what she learns and sees, the coach further connects with the educator's experience and forges a deeper relationship with her. This earns the coach the credibility that she will capitalize on during follow-up reflective discussions, future classroom visits, and group-learning sessions that involve the educator.

Developing a Deep Understanding of Educators' Day-to-Day Experiences

During classroom visits, while the coach is taking a hands-on approach to classroom support, she is simultaneously *observing*— continuously tuning into classroom interactions, processes, and dynamics. These observations ground the coach's work in educators' lived experiences, equipping her with the

Modeling

- Carrying out demonstration lessons
  - For example, modeling an interactive read-aloud
- Exhibiting strategies discussed in group-training sessions (taking advantage of "teachable moments")
  - For example, praising a child's effort, using specific and positive language, interacting respectfully with other educators in the classroom

Collaborating

- Co-teaching
  - For example, supporting the educator in carrying out a plan devised in a group-training session
- Problem solving
  - For example, talking through the educator's in-the-moment questions as she tries a new strategy
- Co-observing
  - For example, noticing children's responses to strategies, along with the educator

Empowering

- Noticing and commending the use of new strategies
  - For example, providing a thumbs-up or enthusiastic, knowing smile (refraining from interrupting the lesson flow by interacting with words)
- Encouraging the use of strategies discussed in group-training sessions
  - For example, when the educator asks the coach for guidance, responding with a prompt or question that supports the educator to recall relevant learning

Relating

- Validating the educator's experience; refraining from judgment
  - For example, after a difficult transition from one activity to the next, expressing how hard these parts of the day can be (for all of us)
- Respecting and adhering to classroom norms and expectations
  - For example, when the educator reminds children that they are responsible for putting away the materials they used, encouraging children to follow this expectation (and not undermining it by putting the materials away for them)
- Helping with classroom routines
  - For example, wiping down tables, preparing materials, and supporting transitions
- Getting to know children in the classroom
  - For example, learning their names and interests, forming caring relationships, and making it known that you, like the teacher, are there to support the rules and activities of the classroom

FIGURE 8.5. Coaching "moves" for the classroom.

insights needed to plan, problem solve, and strategize. Otherwise, the coach's guidance, no matter how research based or useful in other settings, might not be feasible, relevant, or targeted enough to truly support and enhance educators' practices.

Observing during classroom visits is only the first step in developing this deep understanding of educators' day-to-day experiences. The coach must follow up her observations by reflecting on what was observed. Most often, this reflection happens through note taking—formally documenting key observations, and in so doing, sharpening her understanding. These contemporaneous notes create a record of the visit and are important for informing the focus and details of the follow-up reflective conversation between the educator and coach (described in more detail in the sections that follow). Over time the coach will amass a collection of notes that can be used to track an educator's progress and discern any patterns with respect to pressure points in her development and/or even in the classroom. The coach can then begin to answer questions such as: In what areas is the educator demonstrating effort and progress? What might underlie an educator's challenges? How can group-learning sessions better match the educator's needs and context? How is this educator's experience similar to, or different from, her colleagues in our group (or PLC)?

Creating a collection of coaching notes that can serve these purposes does not require copious writing, but it does require the coach to consistently document pertinent details in order to ground her analysis of her visits. In our work, we found that coaching notes were most useful when they included

- logistical information, including the time and date of the observation and the activities and routines observed;
- instances when strategies discussed in the group-learning sessions were applied;
- instances when there were missed opportunities to apply strategies discussed in group-learning sessions; and
- instances when the educator or children experienced a difficulty that is relevant to the goals and content of the professional learning scope and sequence more generally.

In Figures 8.6 and 8.7, we provide sample protocols for documenting observations. When using these protocols, leaders will find that not all classroom visits by coaches lend themselves to addressing every section; only those sections that are helpful and relevant should be completed.

Previsit Notes and Reminders

Planned date and time:

Goals:

My plan:

Classroom Visit

Date: _____ Time: _____ Activity/Routine observed: _____

Postvisit Notes and Reflections
Observed Connections to Group-Learning Sessions

Strategies or activities applied	
Strategies or activities that might have been helpful	
Efforts and progress toward goals	
Challenges	

Considering My Own Practice

What were my own challenges and strengths during this visit?

Preparing for the Follow-Up Conversation

What questions do I have for the educator, and what ideas might I present?

FIGURE 8.6. Observation protocol for connected coaching.

Describing the Classroom Visit

What were your goals and expectations?

What activities and routines took place?

What, if any, ideas or strategies from group-learning sessions were used?

What did you notice children doing?

What did you notice about your practice?

Reflecting on the Visit

- What, specifically, went well? How did your actions contribute to these experiences?

- What, specifically, was challenging? Why do you think these challenges came up?

Linking Reflections to Actions

What will you try next? What ideas or strategies from group-training sessions might be useful?

How can coaching support your plan?

The next coaching visit:
Date and time:
Goals:

FIGURE 8.7. Discussion protocol for connected coaching.

Strategy 2: Collaboratively Reflect and Plan with the Educator

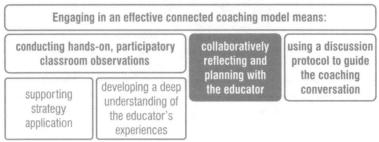

The second strategy for putting connected coaching into practice is engaging in individualized discussions with each educator about the interactions, processes, and instruction that took place during the classroom visit. They quickly follow a coach's visit (ideally within a couple of days) and are paramount to leveraging the classroom visit in ways that enhance educator competencies. As discussed in the previous section, the primary goals of the coach's classroom visits are to support educators' strategy use and to develop a deep understanding of classroom experiences. Follow-up discussions between the coach and educator further these goals, using the shared classroom experience from the visit as a concrete platform for collaborative reflection and planning based on these observations.

In this model, reflection is at the heart of individualized coaching conversations. By *reflection,* we mean careful and thoughtful consideration of the shared classroom experience, with the goal of better understanding, and learning from, the experience. Sharing similarities with Costa and Garmston's (2002) model of *cognitive coaching,* these discussions are a channel through which educators have opportunities to

- reflect on specific moments in the classroom, and
- fine-tune their professional reflection skills.

Why focus on reflection during the coaching discussion? Recall that reflection is an aspect of each and every cornerstone educator competency discussed in Part I (see Figure 8.8). This metacognitive strategy is requisite for self-awareness and intentionality, whether in the realm of emotional, relational, or instructional responses and actions. For example, when educators reflect on their emotional responses, their emotion awareness begins to grow into emotion understanding, and, as such, they begin to identify common times of day or situations when emotional "hot spots" arise and to take the steps necessary for regaining their composure. Similarly, when educators reflect on their use

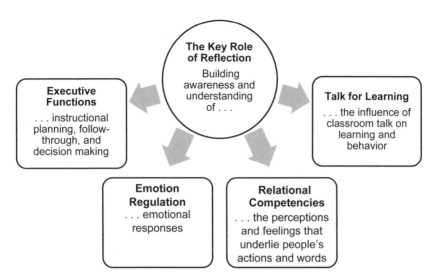

FIGURE 8.8. Revisiting the role of reflection in cornerstone competencies.

of executive functioning strategies, they are forging a deeper understanding of how instructional plans and classroom decision making are linked to children's learning and engagement.

Planning, in and of itself, is a critical component of executive functioning in the classroom, one that is responsive to the needs and goals of the individual educator. As a result of this shared reflection, the coach and educator are poised to plan and problem solve together—to use insights to inform future actions. A plan might be constructed to support any number of cornerstone competencies, whether it is a plan to put emotion management strategies to use, a plan to prompt student conversations at a particular time of day, or a plan for how to better collaborate with a co-teacher.

Voices from the Field
Individualized Coaching Discussions

"The coach helps me set goals for the week and see if I conquered them."

"I was going through a lot, and I opened up with the coach . . . She is very patient and she listened, and it helped tremendously in terms of stress and frustration."

Strategy 3: Use a Discussion Protocol to Guide the Coaching Conversation

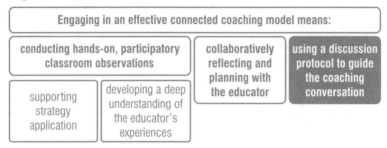

In our work, the coach and educator use a protocol outlined on a shared document that provides a structure for the reflective conversation (see Figure 8.7 for a sample protocol). This document lists a series of steps and questions for the conversation and leaves space for the coach and educator to record their insights. The questions listed on the protocol are directed toward the educator, prompting her to share and reflect before the coach adds her comments to the educator's thoughts. This orientation helps to support the coach's adoption of a partnership approach—one in which both the coach and educator engage in the hard work of reflection and planning, as well as having valuable ideas to share.

The protocol begins by orienting the conversation around the classroom visit. The construction of this honest, shared narrative begins with the educator summarizing the specific events, activities, and interactions that took place during the visit, including what she noticed the children doing; what she noticed about her own instruction and responses; and how, specifically, she enacted the strategies learned during group-training sessions. Then, the coach adds her comments to the educator's observations, ensuring that their perceptions are aligned.

Once the coach and educator have a common understanding of the classroom experience—and this experience is briefly documented on the shared protocol—this shared perspective is the starting point for collaborative reflection. To start, the coach can use broad, reflective prompts, such as

- "What, specifically, went well? How did your actions contribute to these experiences?"
- "What, specifically, was challenging? Why do you think these challenges came up?"

Subsequently, the coach's questions become more targeted, steering the reflective conversation down one of multiple reflection paths. As shown in

Figure 8.9, the conversation might focus on one or more of the cornerstone competencies. The nature of the coach's follow-up prompts, in response to the educator's goals and needs, guide the conversation toward enhancing these competencies. Figure 8.9 provides sample coaching prompts.

The insights garnered from the collaborative reflection process and recorded on the shared coaching-conversation document then become a departure point for formulating a plan that addresses specific classroom needs. For this reason, the final section of the discussion protocol concentrates on planning and problem solving, and this stage can (and should) take multiple paths. For example, if the reflection process focused on categorizing the educator's challenges into those that are within and outside of the educator's control, the coach and educator might use the planning stage of their discussion to talk through how the educator might forecast those challenges within her control and use strategies to prevent them from arising (see Chapter 2). On the other hand, if the educator is concerned that her rising stress levels during tense classroom moments are influencing how she responds (e.g., reacting to children's outbursts with harsh words or threatening consequences that are unreasonable or not implemented), the coach and educator might direct their attention to emotion management strategies (see Chapter 3).

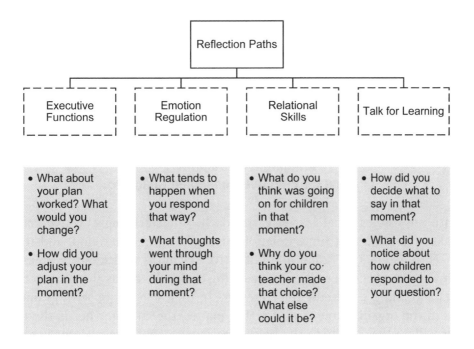

FIGURE 8.9. The individualized coaching conversation: Reflection paths and example coaching prompts.

Whatever the focus, the coach continues to take an approach characterized by partnership and connection. The coach frames the conversation as one between experts, communicating that both the educator and the coach are valuable and can offer useful insights and ideas. As such, during the reflective process, the coach actively listens in order to

- seek clarification (i.e., asking questions, such as "Can you tell me more about what you mean?");
- communicate her understanding of what the educator shares (e.g., paraphrasing what she hears and expressing empathy; explaining, for example, "It sounds like when the children _____, you felt _____."); and
- add to what the educator highlights by (prudently) putting some of her own insights on the table (e.g., "I also noticed that _____. What do you think?")

Then, when coplanning, the coach continues to enact a partnership approach by

- prompting the educator for ideas (i.e., "How might you address that?"; "Let's look back at strategies we've talked about during our group sessions. Which ones might be helpful in this situation?"); offering suggestions (e.g., "What if you tried . . . ?"); and learning from the educator how the coach might support her plans moving forward, (i.e., "What can I do during my next visit to your classroom that would help?"; "How can we use group sessions to help you with your goals?").

Bringing It All Together:
Leading for Effective Connected Coaching

As with any professional learning approach, implementing effective coaching takes planning and time. Relationships take time to develop, and if the coach is to assess individual and collective strengths and identify areas on which to concentrate as part of the learning cycle, she needs the time to fully understand and get to know the educators in their classroom settings and as adults in the organization. And, for that matter, the educator needs the time to learn about the coach's in-the-field experience, acquire respect for her, and develop trust so that the relationship can be fruitful for the early educator, and ultimately, the children. Early education leaders can encourage this work by acknowledging and protecting this time investment and by remaining patient while an important foundation is being laid.

It is also important to recognize that a coach is not an evaluator. In other words, the connected coaching relationship is a means of building educator capacity in a safe, constructive way—not a means of figuring out an educator's weaknesses and then sharing the information with education leaders for evaluative purposes. Early education leaders can preserve the sanctity of this relationship by not asking questions specific to the caliber or performance of any one educator—and instead maintain connections by being present at professional learning sessions or establishing weekly or biweekly meetings with a coach—to remain informed, involved, and supportive, while not putting others in a potentially awkward or vulnerable position.

Early education leaders should also bear in mind that a coach may need to rely on them to engage in an effective connected coaching model with the educators at her setting. After all, every setting is different—and so are all people! An early education leader should be willing to support the coach in all aspects of designing and implementing approaches to professional learning (see Chapter 6)—from planning (think cohesive, ongoing, and anchored in site-level data) to carrying out the details (think coverage and providing a consistent space for meetings). Every effective coach has an early education leader who has her back.

Finally, we also recognize that, due to resource and staffing constraints, the leader's site may not have an "actual" coach. An early education leader can certainly facilitate PLCs and assume the coaching role—just keep these points from Chapter 7 and 8 about trust, respect, and evaluation in mind from the start. There are many examples of strong center directors, for example, carrying out effective coaching.

As we look to close this book, in Chapter 9 we assess readiness for getting started on a system of professional learning that fully supports educators—including getting connected coaching and group-learning sessions up and running. But, first, we encourage leaders to use the self-study tool provided in Figure 8.10 to think about coaching at their site(s).

In connected coaching models, the coach . . .	What do you notice about your existing coaching model?
conducts hands-on participatory classroom observations.	
supports strategy application and connects to PLC work.	
develops a deep appreciation of the early educator's experience.	
collaboratively reflects with the educator.	
collaboratively plans with the educator.	
guides the coaching conversation using a discussion protocol.	

What patterns do you notice?

FIGURE 8.10. Self-study tool for connected coaching.

PART III

Conclusion

CHAPTER 9

Leading a 21st-Century Early Education Setting

Supporting Educators to Support Children

It is June. Melinda, the director of the Explorations Early Learning Center, has just left a PreK classroom. She pauses a moment to reflect as she sits down at her desk, smiling to herself as she thinks about the visit. At the point when Melinda arrived, Maria had been reading to the children; there was so much talk—sharing thoughts and feelings among the children and also with Maria—that Melinda smiles again. The children were so engaged. It was clear that Maria was applying everything she has been working on this year, asking great questions and giving children lots of opportunities to respond. Meanwhile, Jada had been working with Anthony, who asked to get up from the rug area, self-advocating for a body break. The two of them were sitting together, doing some calm breathing. "You made a good choice for yourself when your body was tired of sitting," she said. Jada looked up at Melinda and winked, saying "This actually helps me, too!"

Melinda reflects with satisfaction on the evident progress made over the last year, which had not been without struggle. She thinks about the initial pushback and reticence she observed when she first brought Karen, the coach, on board. She knows that these professional relationships are still definitely in the making, but a foundation of trust has clearly been established. Melinda looks at her calendar—and ahead to the next academic year. She starts to think about the plan for the fall.

For leaders like Melinda there are few experiences as satisfying and motivating as a moment that validates and reinforces capacity-building efforts designed to improve learning and teaching. Melinda watches an educator thoughtfully engage children in quality talk around a text, giving her children an opportunity to share with each other, connect to the text, and develop their cognitive skills. Melinda also catches a glimpse of emotionally responsive teaching, as Jada uses positive language and praise (see Chapter 5) with Anthony when he demonstrates emotional awareness and understanding and is able to use a strategy to manage his behavior, or self-regulate. Melinda notes that, in turn, Maria responds empathically (see Chapter 3), and notably, makes the link between Anthony's choice and the benefit of the calming technique for herself!

This year of work was focused on enhancing key educator competencies and strategies (see Part I), supported by the professional development structures and processes we discuss in this book (see Chapter 6). The group-learning sessions provided crucial opportunities for collaboration and reflection (see Chapter 7), and connected coaching bridged the group-based learning to individual educators' practices (see Chapter 8).

As this vignette suggests, adult learning and improvements in practice are achieved only with a lot of hard work, persistence, patience, and, as we all know (!), the motivation of everyone involved to work through some challenges and bumps along the way. For leaders like Melinda, the only way to get there is through a tremendous amount of planning—both ahead of the work and in response to the work. Consistent with the professional learning we have described in this book, Melinda has engaged in this kind of thoughtful planning, and she has navigated the process of change and relationship management among adults along the way. To be sure, roadblocks are common and expected on the path to improved teaching and learning. But the benefits for everyone are clear. Enhanced competencies among educators in the domains of executive functions, emotion awareness and management, relational skills, and talk for learning enhance their sense of efficacy and their confidence; meanwhile their stress levels and vulnerability to burnout are reduced significantly. And all reap these benefits before we even highlight the positive effects for the learners in their classrooms—these children, too, are likely to experience a boost in these same competencies—their executive functions, relational skills, management of their emotions and behavior, and language development. As a result, their early learning and development overall is enhanced.

Recognizing and agreeing that the key to increasing educator capacity and effectiveness in the classroom rests on the professional supports offered is only the first, very small step in the process. What comes next is a fundamental shift in how settings are organized to provide these learning opportunities in vivo—not as events or instances that are simply called professional development. In the next sections, we guide early education leaders as they get started in implementing a tailored professional development *system* that is responsive to their context's needs.

In this final chapter, we help the early education leader to design and implement the different aspects of professional development described in this book—ultimately putting in place a system of ongoing professional learning. Specifically, we present and describe a learning cycle that is integral to this system. We also identify common roadblocks that leaders will likely encounter, and we highlight common responses to reform that actually act as barriers to quality. We close with additional resources for taking on an improvement effort such as this one.

A Five-Part Learning Cycle
for Effective Design and Implementation

At its core, getting to meaningful change is ultimately about implementation—and getting to effective implementation demands, among other things, processes to support and reinforce the work of the adults: the trying, practicing, troubleshooting, and learning. Good processes also fuel the growth mindset that is needed to achieve results. For this reason, we introduce a learning cycle that serves as a touchstone for improvement work. We deploy this learning cycle in all of our work, whether it is site-based work with educators, executive education for leaders, or assisting graduate students in translating their work into practice and/or policy. Not only does the cycle guide professional learning in concrete ways, it also represents a habit of mind that can and should be cultivated among adults. The learning cycle (see Figure 9.1) consists of five action steps that build on one another: 1. *Notice*, 2. *Analyze*, 3. *Build Knowledge*, 4. *Plan*, and 5. *Try*. In following sections, we describe each part of the cycle.

Notice

This first step focuses on helping participants examine their settings with fresh eyes—taking a step back, so to speak. In this step, the focus is on observing and documenting specific challenges or growth areas in daily work, always using data, as outlined in Chapter 6. After all, it is only through data and documentation that patterns or trends are identified, and to make the best use of time and effort, professional learning efforts should be anchored in real challenges and areas for improvement as identified by these patterns and trends. Noticing through the use of data can take many forms with respect to the kind of data (e.g., daily classroom logs, child assessment, site-level health and safety data) and the area of focus (e.g., student behavior, student learning, classroom routines and activities, and educator stress levels). These data can be informal

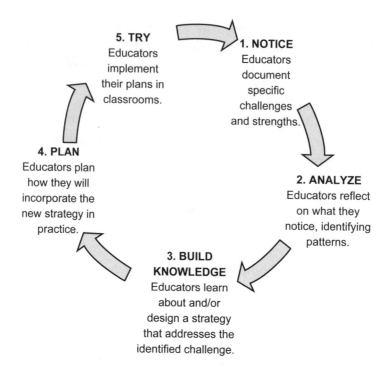

FIGURE 9.1. The five-part learning cycle.

and very efficient to collect but nevertheless will add up to patterns and trends; for example, a quick Post-it Note with a rating of the engagement level of children in a daily activity over several weeks or the educator's level of stress during a particular event or periodically, along with the time and date (see Figure 9.2 for an example).

Analyze

While so much of the daily work in early education feels hurried—lesson planning, moving from one activity to the next with the goal of maximizing learning time, making daily leadership decisions and changes to benefit learning and teaching—it is hard to imagine how slowing down to create the habit of analysis could actually increase effectiveness. But the bottom line is that meaningful change can only take place within a system that values planning, analysis, and more planning, to build teacher capacity and provide high-quality settings for our youngest learners! In this second step, leaders and their teams therefore take the data gathered in the first step and analyze what they have noticed. Here they work to identify and think carefully about what might

Name: _____ Date: _____

1. **What is one moment today that went especially well or that you feel happy about?**	
When did it happen (e.g., center time, morning meeting, free play outside)?	
What were the children doing at this time? What about your co-teacher or floating teacher?	
What do you think made that moment go so well?	
2. **What is one moment today that was especially difficult?**	
When did it happen (e.g., center time, morning meeting, free play outside)?	
What were the children doing at this time? What about your co-teacher or floating teacher?	
What do you think made that moment difficult?	

FIGURE 9.2. Sample documentation sheet for the purpose of noticing.

underlie the patterns and trends in the data, or specific challenges, that have been observed. The more analysis that occurs—in other words, the more significant the "step back"—the higher the likelihood that key trends in behavior and thought will be identified. In our work, analysis was critical for leaders and educators, but especially so for the coaches, who, in order to be most effective, need to reflect constructively on the work of the educators they support, so that they can respond to needs as they arise and adjust the course of action accordingly.

Build Knowledge

The third step focuses on identifying the knowledge building that ought to take place in response to the identified area of growth and challenge—whether to enhance and deepen existing knowledge or acquire new knowledge of a particular skill, competency, or strategy altogether. In our work, PLC meetings (see Chapter 7) served as the arena for developing background knowledge, frequently accompanied by professional readings, videos, and discussion to establish a collective understanding of a topic or issue. For example, when focusing on the early educator's relational competencies, before moving to strategies, we addressed how relational skills affect classroom management, the quality of relationships in the classroom, and children's own relational skills (see Chapter 4). While often in early education, the field targets a specific strategy for implementation, taking the time to build background knowledge is very important. It gives early educators the *why*, and it often establishes buy-in required for the impending work. It can also promote professional autonomy, as educators, mindful of their needs and context, can think about additional routes to the desired outcome, even if they are focused on learning and implementing a specific strategy. Gaining more background knowledge guides educators in knowing what to look for and supports reflecting on their work with children and colleagues.

Plan

The fourth step is to plan *how* a new strategy will be incorporated into daily work and/or practice. This planning can take various forms. For a leader, it may occur within the leadership team's regular meeting. In a PLC with connected coaching, for example, educators apply background knowledge and plan application of the strategy. In all formats, we strongly recommend the use of planning tools to support the use of the new strategy in daily work (See Chapter 2 for tools that support the instructional planning process.)

Try

The last step is to take action to implement the plan! In a scenario with coaching, it is, of course, crucial that the coach be available to participate and observe the educator in action when she is ready—especially because the coach is instrumental in carrying out all the other steps in this ongoing improvement cycle. In many cases, for example, the change starts with the educator and coach working together in the "notice and analyze" stages when pressure points, challenges, and areas for growth are identified. This implementation stage also affords the opportunity for the leader and/or coach, or others who are in a leadership or support role, to continue to notice and analyze—and consider the next steps.

Having enumerated these five steps, two highly important points are worth remembering. First, the use of the cycle is ultimately iterative and ongoing. The work of achieving meaningful change does not simply involve one run through the cycle. For example, when trying a new strategy, the learning community will get to Step 5 and then reengage in Step 1, this time noticing both positive and negative changes that have resulted from implementation. These observations should be documented as part of the process. For any continuous improvement process to be effective, teams need to repeat the cycle regularly. Ultimately, the cycle of learning and inquiry should become a mindset that is

Building Knowledge as a Starting Point in the Five-Part Cycle
Developing Teacher Readiness to Notice

Melinda, the director of the Explorations Early Learning Center, is examining her formal observation tools and notes from classroom visits and notices a pattern: most activities in classroom activity time are assigned to children. Children are told which centers to visit at particular times. "Providing choice is so beneficial to child development and helps foster interest and autonomy. I wonder why we aren't providing children with more choices during activity time?" Melinda then plans with Karen, the Center's coach, to build the background knowledge of her teachers around the importance of incorporating choice into the PreK classroom and its cognitive and emotional benefits at an upcoming PLC. Melinda is surprised to learn that many of the early educators at the Center didn't know about the importance of choice. At the PLC, they each make a plan to incorporate choice into activity time, and when they try their plans out, Karen visits the classroom to observe and participate. The educators notice what went well—overall, students were more engaged and motivated. They also notice some challenges: several students stayed at the dramatic play center the entire time. Together, teachers reflect on what they notice and design a strategy to improve upon the challenges.

part of daily work, whether for a reflective leader or for a practitioner seeking to both solve problems and maximize impact. Second, it is important to note that the entry point to this cycle does not always have to be at the noticing step. In fact it may be more helpful for some early educators to begin by building knowledge. In some cases, effective noticing depends on teacher readiness and knowledge about what to even look for. Regardless of which step is the starting point, it is important to repeat the entire cycle systematically and continuously.

Common Roadblocks along the Path to Improvement

To be sure, realizing meaningful change and growth mindsets does not happen overnight—and it is important to recognize that the path toward quality will certainly be marked with obstacles. In what follows, we identify some of the most common challenges and potential roadblocks, as well as resources that might be helpful if they are encountered, recognizing that every setting is different and each set of challenges is uniquely varied with respect to issues such as the characteristics, stakeholders, and policies involved.

Common Roadblock 1: Managing Unease That Comes with Change

Understanding any improvement process as a change process, learning how to develop commitment among those who might oppose the change and working toward transforming the culture are important processes to contemplate—and also to plan for. Specifically, a common issue for early education leaders, and many education leaders more generally, is managing the unease that comes with any new initiative or reform effort. This is especially the case when the initiative focuses on making new demands of educators and/or exposes adults' daily work and practice in ways that likely, at least at first, feel uncomfortable. In addition, designing and implementing a new system of professional learning that is the subject of this chapter (and this book) can instill a sense of unease or dissatisfaction in educators, who have to rethink and reframe the way they participate in professional development. What we have described and recommend stands in very stark contrast to the stand-and-deliver "training" model that educators are most familiar with—one in which they are able to be passive learners, to take it all in, and then decide what, if anything, they will bring from the training into their classrooms.

In our experience, arriving at the professional learning system and culture we present involves implementing these new structures and processes, maintaining a very strong commitment to consistency, and refraining entirely from an evaluative or impatient stance in carrying out the action steps. At the core, consider the many systems in place to have the voice of early educators heard and valued as part of the process. For example, in the structures of PLCs (see Chapter 7) and connected coaching (see Chapter 8) there are excellent opportunities for collaborative learning, personalized professional learning, and an outlet for early educators' concerns to be acknowledged and responded to. Further, emphasizing patterns in site-level data (see Chapter 6) helps remind teams of educators that all are responsible for a population of children and that the work is focused on collective investment and improvement.

Common Roadblock 2: Addressing and Supporting Conflict Resolution among Adult Learners

Many early education leaders entered the profession because of a connection to the overall mission of getting children off to a good start by boosting their early learning and development. For some, working with and learning along-side adults is simply a means to our shared goal of supporting children through high-quality early learning environments, not necessarily an end in itself. And because many leaders' strengths relate to early childhood education or at the broader level, effective policymaking, there exists a common knowledge gap in the area of adult learning and development. Yet the work, and success, of leaders depend entirely on effectively working with adults—and this entails having strong skills in the areas of collaboration, management, and professional support. As part of the implementation of an effective system of professional learning specifically, the skills in the domain of working with adults include being proactive in identifying and supporting resolution of everyday pressure points and conflicts that are likely to arise among colleagues as part of an intensely collaborative, relational process.

One way to develop these skills is to be aware of adults as learners. Although adult development looks and feels different from that of children, it is important to remember that adults too are still learning and developing. And taking care to recognize that adult learning is different from an educator's pedagogical understanding is an important step. For example, it is important for leaders to know that adults are motivated by being involved in planning their own learning, to know that learning should be relevant and centered on a problem, and to understand that, as with our young learners, an experiential element is key to development (Knowles, 1984). Additionally, thinking about adults' varied styles of learning, having different strategies for approaching conflict and offering effective feedback, and pushing oneself to take others' perspectives are important points to consider when guiding adults through professional learning experiences.

Finally, further developing emotion awareness and management is vital in working with adults and ultimately influences children's outcomes. As we describe in Chapter 3, children learn from and respond to the way adults deal with stress; therefore, helping adults to deal with everyday stress in constructive, reflective ways will benefit them in their relationships with other adults and with children.

Common Roadblock 3: Weak Coordination and Cohesion among Professional Learning Opportunities

A third potential roadblock toward building early educator capacity involves a lack of coordination and cohesion among the learning opportunities being offered—and how educators often fail to understand the ways these fit together and add up to a larger goal.

As discussed in Chapter 6, much of today's professional development training is too infrequent, too brief, and/or disconnected from daily practice and/or a larger goal and plan for site-based improvement to meaningfully alter practice. We also remind leaders that learning *about* a practice and successfully *implementing* that practice in a classroom are two different accomplishments for early educators (Zaslow et al., 2010, 2011). Therefore, we stress the importance of designing effective professional development trainings that reflect the 21st-century model described in this book. Thoughtful planning and reflection around a specific goal, as well as deploying the learning cycle consistently and continually to support improvement, are essential to preventing and addressing this roadblock. Specifically, a few key reminders are worth noting.

• *Build a shared understanding of a specific goal.* All stakeholders and participants within the learning community need a shared understanding of the specific goal, from the beginning, to achieve buy-in and collaboration. (For a discussion, see Chapter 6.)

• *Ensure strategic planning.* We cannot stress enough the importance of planning. To this end, the sample scope-and-sequence figures and macro-level planning tools we provide in Appendix 9.1 at the end of this chapter are designed to help. Figure 9.3 shows sample PLC topics to be explored during a module. Figure 9.4 is a sample sequence of professional learning experiences (organized by module and further broken down into PLCs) for site-level work. Figures 9.5 through 9.9 support planning PLC topics and content and a cohesive sequence.

● *Prioritize time to do the work well.* We value what we make time for! When leaders do not take the time to do the work consistently, it sends the message that the work is not as important as perhaps has been discussed. The gap between talking about priorities and taking action is something to watch for. Progress and impact start with setting aside the time—it signals professionalism, establishes cohesion, and supports the commitment to working toward a common goal.

● *Allow educators time for practice with the right supports.* Motivating educators to consistently use new strategies is a big challenge. For this reason, we turn to the learning cycle (see Chapter 6), which includes supported practice and application from another adult (e.g., coach or facilitator), who is also entrenched in the daily work.

Common Roadblock 4: Providing Structures without Processes

Whether crafting state policies and strategies to support the early education workforce, directing a PreK center, or serving as a head teacher, these leaders in early education are likely thinking about how to enhance foundational competencies among the early educators they serve and work with. In planning this leadership work, a critical distinction to consider is that between *structures* and *processes.* Structures are the tangible, concrete parts of any plan or strategy that can be put in place and that we can see daily in our work. For example, curriculum materials, staff meetings, assessments, and documents that are included in the PLC's activities. Processes, on the other hand, are not tangible and not easily seen, but they are what make the structures effective. They are the interactions and practices that result from using a structure well; it is the processes—not the structures—that are tied to continuous learning. For example, let's consider the tools educators can use to document their emotional responses (see Chapter 3). In this case, the actual tool, a type of logging tool, is the structure. The processes include the noticing, reflecting, troubleshooting, discussion with colleagues, facilitator feedback, and the act of making a change—all of which were made possible because of a set of structures that were set in place.

What is most important to understand is that *every structure needs a process,* and *every process needs a structure.* And educators need both for effective supports and continuous improvement. Unfortunately, however, the tendency is to base our improvement plans and expectations on structures alone. The field is not yet in the habit of attending to and articulating the processes that go with structures. Therefore, for leaders, the pitfall to avoid is giving educators a tool or a set of tools and asking them to use them without also putting in place the processes that make them useful platforms for supporting planning, collaboration, reflection, and improvement. This lack of attention to process is a key reason why the results of a change effort are often disappointing. It is the combination of structures *and* processes together that create meaningful, lasting change.

Bringing It All Together: Leadership for 21st-Century Early Education Settings

Improving the quality of our early learning environments begins with investing in the educators who work so closely with our youngest learners each day. And a primary investment in meeting today's context and educators' needs is a new model of professional learning—one that focuses on enhancing educator competencies and embeds learning cycles, facilitated group-based learning opportunities, the use of protocols and tools for strategic planning and collaboration, and ongoing support for practice and application in sites everywhere. The new model also entails fostering a growth mindset among the adults focused on daily teaching and learning, who see opportunities in meeting a challenge and have a constructive, positive orientation to pressure points and roadblocks along the way. As they go about the important daily work of leading high-quality learning environments, today's early education leaders are invited to empower their colleagues, other leaders, and early educators to take up this work and adopt this mindset. In so doing, they will cut a clearer path toward strong learning and development, and more children will have the opportunity to access high-quality early education experiences.

APPENDIX 9.1. Scope-and-Sequence and Macro-Level Planning Tools

Professional Learning Community	What will educators work on?	Why does this matter?
PLC # 9: Analyzing the classroom stress spiral	Examining the links among thoughts, emotions, and behaviors in one's common responses to stress	When educators can identify how thoughts influence their emotions and behaviors, they can begin establishing healthier thought patterns.
PLC # 10: Introducing the brain's role in stress	Bringing information together from prior workshops to understand the brain's role in stress	Supporting educators to understand the brain's role in stress universalizes common responses to stress, reducing feelings of isolation.
PLC # 11: How our brains respond to stress	Identifying the ways in which different parts of the brain are activated during the stress response	Teaching the parts of the brain promotes educators' abilities to shift from reactive to proactive responses to stress.
PLC # 12: Shifting our thinking to manage stress	Using healthy thought patterns as a strategy for activating the brain's adaptive stress response	Because thoughts influence emotions and behaviors, educators' use of healthy thought patterns promotes adaptive responses to classroom stress.

FIGURE 9.3. Sample PLC topics for Module 3: Applying knowledge from brain science to manage classroom stress.

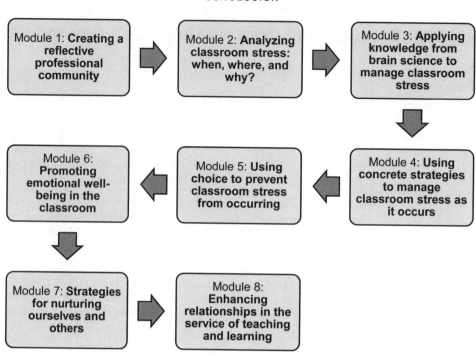

FIGURE 9.4. Sample sequence of professional learning experiences to build early educator competencies.

Professional Learning Community	What will educators work on?	Why does this matter?
PLC 1:		
PLC 2:		
PLC 3:		
PLC 4:		

FIGURE 9.5. Sample PLC planning tool.

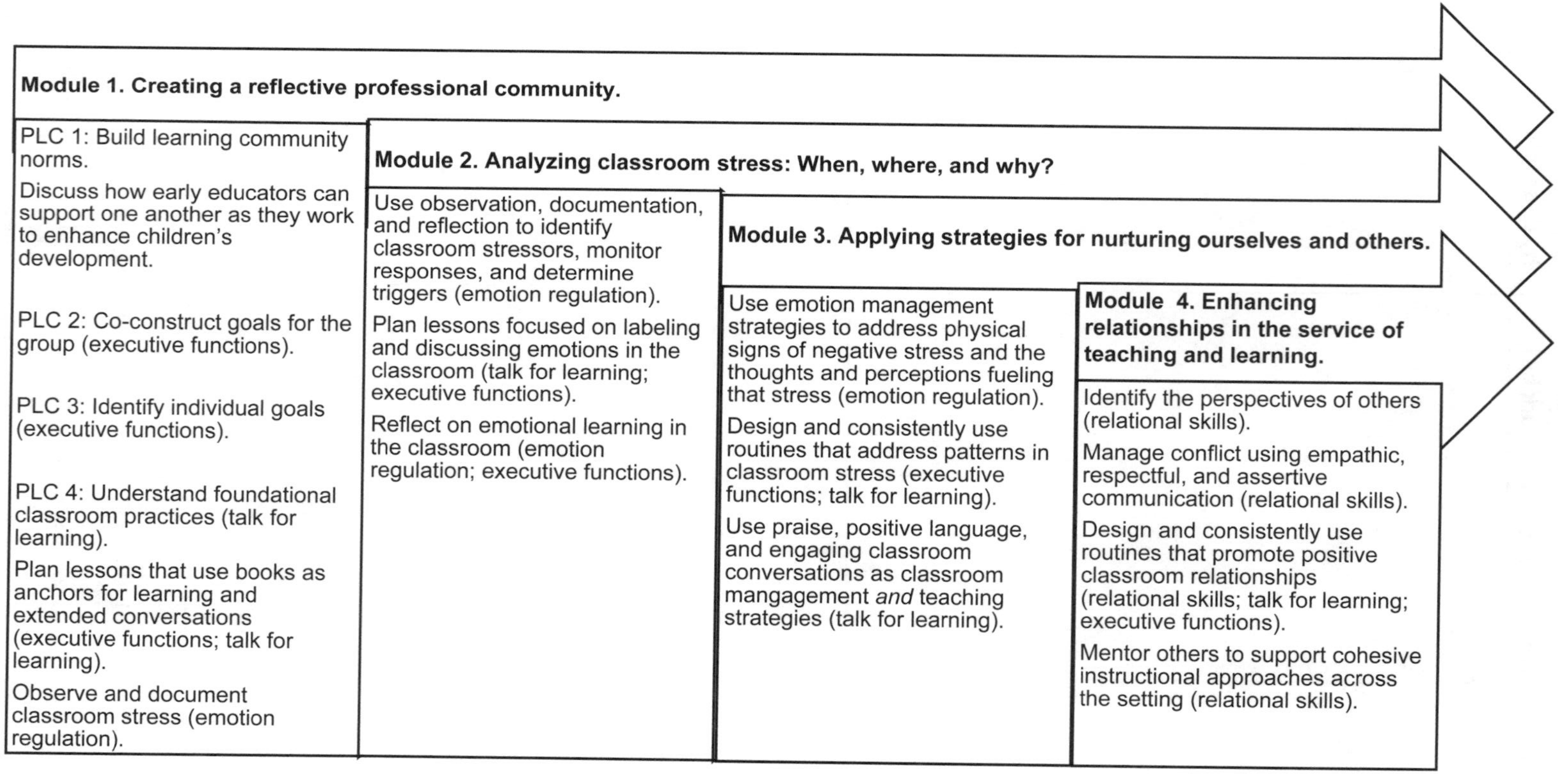

Module 1. Creating a reflective professional community.

Module 2. Analyzing classroom stress: When, where, and why?

Module 3. Applying strategies for nurturing ourselves and others.

Module 4. Enhancing relationships in the service of teaching and learning.

PLC 1: Build learning community norms.

Discuss how early educators can support one another as they work to enhance children's development.

PLC 2: Co-construct goals for the group (executive functions).

PLC 3: Identify individual goals (executive functions).

PLC 4: Understand foundational classroom practices (talk for learning).

Plan lessons that use books as anchors for learning and extended conversations (executive functions; talk for learning).

Observe and document classroom stress (emotion regulation).

Use observation, documentation, and reflection to identify classroom stressors, monitor responses, and determine triggers (emotion regulation).

Plan lessons focused on labeling and discussing emotions in the classroom (talk for learning; executive functions).

Reflect on emotional learning in the classroom (emotion regulation; executive functions).

Use emotion management strategies to address physical signs of negative stress and the thoughts and perceptions fueling that stress (emotion regulation).

Design and consistently use routines that address patterns in classroom stress (executive functions; talk for learning).

Use praise, positive language, and engaging classroom conversations as classroom management *and* teaching strategies (talk for learning).

Identify the perspectives of others (relational skills).

Manage conflict using empathic, respectful, and assertive communication (relational skills).

Design and consistently use routines that promote positive classroom relationships (relational skills; talk for learning; executive functions).

Mentor others to support cohesive instructional approaches across the setting (relational skills).

FIGURE 9.6. Sample sequence of cohesive PLCs.

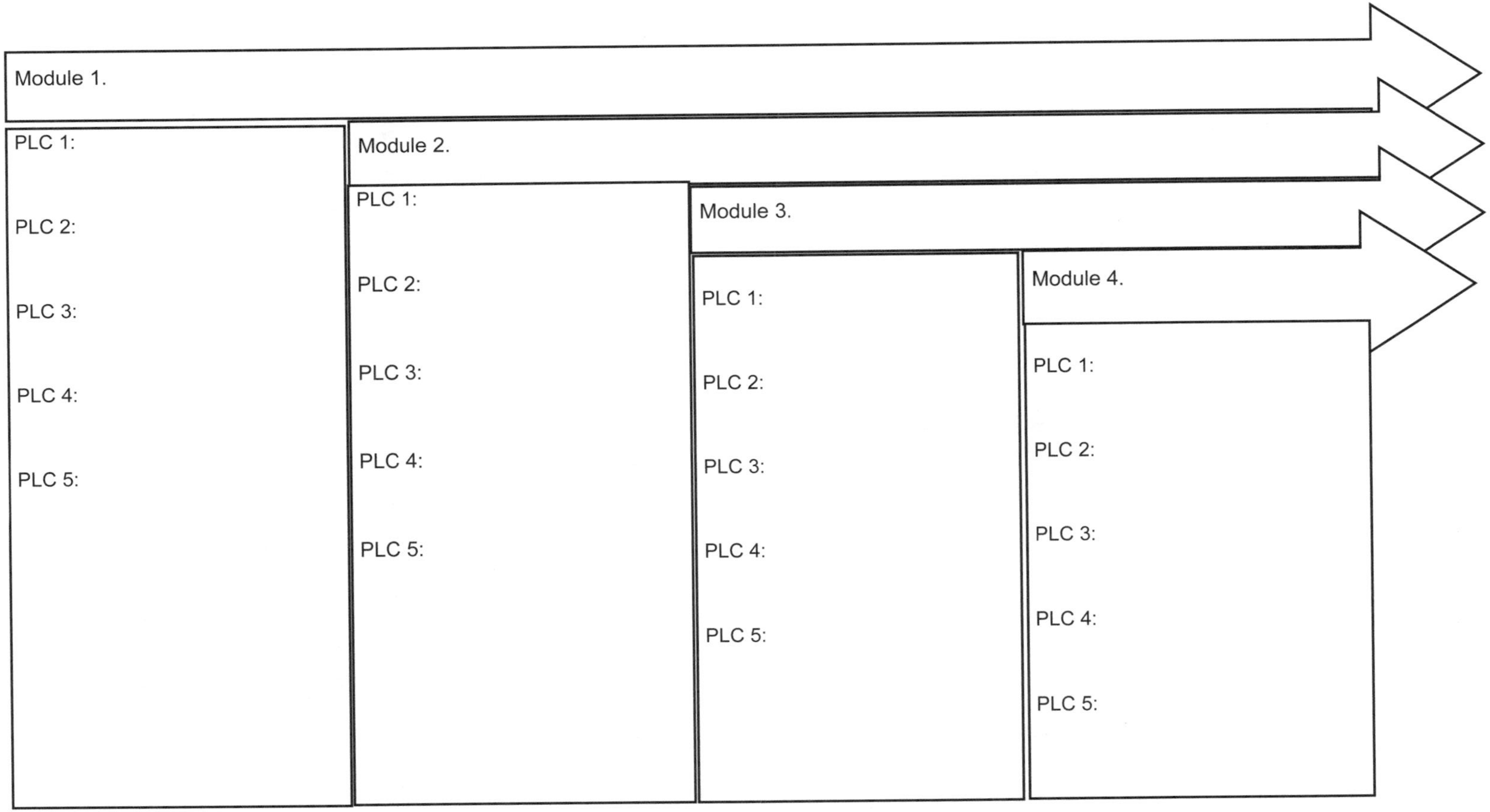

FIGURE 9.7. Sample template for planning scope and sequence of educator competencies across PLCs in each module.

PLC # 4: _Noticing how we respond to classroom interactions_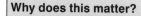

What will educators work on?	**Why does this matter?**
Beginning to use <u>noticing</u> and <u>analyzing</u> as tools for monitoring reactive and proactive responses to classroom interactions. →	_Constructively discussing educators' varied responses to classroom interactions increases their self-awareness about times when they need more support._

Warm-up journal prompt: _Write down one thing you noticed about the children's self-portrait drawings this week._

Materials:
- _The <u>Big 5</u> poster_
- _<u>My Many Colored Days</u> book_
- _<u>Think–Pair–Share</u> bookmark_

> **Facilitator tip/reminder:**
> _Educators will all have a varying level of understanding and experience in using basic principles of child development. Be sure to take all possible levels into consideration when introducing the <u>Big 5</u>._

Workshop Components:

1. **Debrief the self-portrait activity.**
   - _Discuss with educators how the self-portrait activity went with children, using the debrief protocol._

   - _Ask educators what they noticed about the children's self-portrait drawings (revisiting the warm up journal prompt)._

2. **Introduce the _Big 5_ and review the first two items.**
   - _Explain that in our work together it is important that we all have the same understanding of what the latest research tells us about child development._

   - _Tell educators that we will be working with five basic principles and using them as a framework._

   - _Introduce the first two principles: <u>Learning is social</u> and <u>Praise is specific and frequent</u>._

3. **Introduce labeling and expression of feelings, using the read-aloud _My Many Colored Days_.**
   - _Ask educators to do another think–pair–share with their students, using <u>My Many Colored Days</u>; this think–pair–share will focus on discussing emotions._

   - _Explain that children learn to manage their emotions when we support and teach children how to talk about them._

FIGURE 9.8. Sample content for PLC activities.

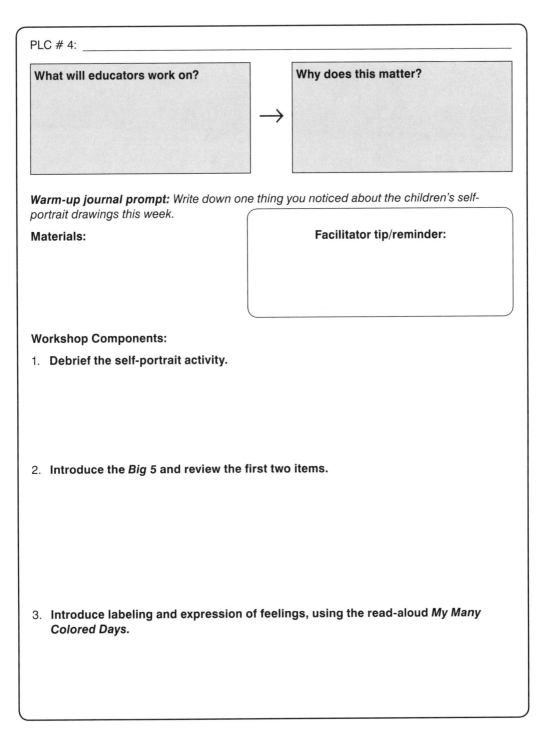

FIGURE 9.9. Sample template for planning PLC content.

References

Badanes, L. S., Dmitrieva, J., & Watamura, S. E. (2012). Understanding cortisol reactivity across the day at child care: The potential buffering role of secure attachments to caregivers. *Early Childhood Research Quarterly, 27*(1), 156–165.

Barnett, W. S. (1995). Long-term effects of early childhood programs on cognitive and school outcomes. *Future of Children, 5*(3), 25–50.

Barnett, W. S., & Nores, M. (2012). *Estimated participation and hours in early care and education by type of arrangement and income at ages 2 to 4 in 2010: NIEER working paper.* New Brunswick, NJ: National Institute for Early Education Research.

Boudett, K., & City, E. A. (2014). *Meeting wise: Making the most of collaborative time for educators.* Cambridge, MA: Harvard Education Press

Bowers, E. P., & Vasilyeva, M. (2011). The relation between teacher input and lexical growth of preschoolers. *Applied Psycholinguistics, 32*(1), 221–241.

Brooks-Gunn, J., & Duncan, G. (1997). The effects of poverty on children. *The Future of Children, 7*(2), 55–71.

Bryk, A., Camburn, E., & Louis, K. S. (1999). Professional community in Chicago elementary schools: Facilitating factors and organizational consequences. *Educational Administration Quarterly, 35*(5), 751–781.

Carle, E. (1984). *The mixed-up chameleon.* New York: HarperCollins.

Carlock, R. (2011). *Executive functions: A review of the literature to inform practice and policy.* Cambridge, MA: Harvard Center on the Developing Child.

Costa, A., & Garmston, R. (2002). *Cognitive coaching: A foundation for renaissance schools.* Norwood, MA: Christopher Gordon.

Curtis, J. L., & Cornell, L. (1998). *Today I feel silly and other moods that make my day.* New York: HarperCollins.

Darling-Hammond, L., Wei, R. C., & Johnson, C. M. (2009). Teacher preparation and teacher learning: A changing policy landscape. In G. Sykes, B. Schneider, & D. N. Plank (Eds.), *The handbook of education policy research* (pp. 613–636). Washington DC: American Educational Research Association.

Denham, S. A., Bassett, H. H., & Zinsser, K. (2012). Early childhood teachers as socializers of young children's emotional competence. *Early Childhood Education Journal, 40*(3), 137–143.

Diamond, A. (2006). Bootstrapping conceptual deduction using physical connection: Rethinking frontal cortex. *Trends in Cognitive Sciences, 10*(5), 212–218.

Dickinson, D. K., & Porche, M. V. (2011). Relation between language experiences in preschool classrooms and children's kindergarten and fourth-grade language and reading abilities. *Child Development, 82*(3), 870–886.

Duke, N. K. (2014). *Inside information: Developing powerful readers and writers of informational text through project-based instruction.* New York: Scholastic Teaching Resources.

Epstein, A. (2014). *The intentional teacher: Choosing the best strategies for young children's learning* (rev. ed.). Washington, DC: National Association for the Education of Young Children.

Gámez, P. B., & Levine, S. C. (2013). Oral language skills of Spanish-speaking English language learners: The impact of high-quality native language exposure. *Applied Psycholinguistics, 34*(4), 673–696.

Goddard, Y. L., Goddard, R. D., & Tschannen-Moran, M. (2007). A theoretical and empirical investigation of teacher collaboration for school improvement and student achievement in public elementary schools. *Teachers College Record, 109*(4), 877–896.

Grant, R., Gracy, D., Goldsmith, G., Shapiro, A., & Redlener, I. E. (2013). Twenty-five years of child and family homelessness: Where are we now? *American Journal of Public Health, 103*(S2), e1–e10.

Harms, T., Cryer, D., & Clifford, R. (2003). *Infant/Toddler Environment Rating Scale—Revised edition.* New York: Teachers College Press.

Henkes, K. (1986). *A weekend with Wendell.* Hong Kong: South China Printing.

Howes, C., & Spieker, S. (2016). Attachment relationships in the context of multiple caregivers. In J. Cassidy & P. R. Shaver (Eds.), *Handbook of attachment: Theory, research, and clinical applications* (pp. 314–329). New York: Guilford Press.

Huttenlocher, J., Vasilyeva, M., Cymerman, E., & Levine, S. (2002). Language input and child syntax. *Cognitive Psychology, 45*(3), 337–374.

Institute of Medicine and the National Research Council. (2015). *Transforming the workforce for children birth through age 8: A unifying foundation.* Washington, DC: National Academy Press.

Jennings, P. A., & Greenberg, M. T. (2009). The prosocial classroom: Teacher social and emotional competence in relation to student and classroom outcomes. *Review of Educational Research, 79*(1), 491–525.

Jones, R. C. (1991). *Matthew and Tilly.* New York: Puffin Books.

Jones, S. M., & Bouffard, S. M. (2012). Social and emotional learning in schools: From programs to strategies. *Society for Research in Child Development, Social Policy Rapport, 26*(4), 3–22.

Jones, S. M., Bouffard, S. M., & Weissbourd, R. (2013). Educators' social and emotional skills vital to learning. *Phi Delta Kappan, 94*(8), 62–65.

Joseph, G., & Strain, P. (2004). Building positive relationship with young children. *Young Exceptional Children, 7*(4), 21–28.

Kachenmeister, C. (1989). *On Monday when it rained.* Boston: Houghton Mifflin.

Knowles, M. (1984). *The adult learner: A neglected species* (3rd ed.). Houston, TX: Gulf.

Leahy, R. L. (2003). *Cognitive therapy techniques: A practitioner's guide.* New York: Guilford Press.

Lieberman, A., & Miller, L. (2011). Learning communities: The starting point for professional learning is in schools and classrooms. *Journal of Staff Development, 32*(4), 16–20.

Lieberman, A., & Miller, L. (2014). Teachers as professionals: Evolving definitions of staff development. In L. Martin, S. Kragler, D. Quatroche, & K. Bauserman (Eds.) *Handbook of professional development in education: Successful models and practices PreK–12* (pp. 3–21). New York: Guilford Press.

Mashburn, A. J., Pianta, R. C., Hamre, B. K., Downer, J. T., Barbarin, O. A., Bryant, D., et al. (2008). Measures of classroom quality in pre-kindergarten and children's development of academic, language, and social skills. *Child Development, 79*(3), 732–749.

Maurer, M., & Brackett, M. A. (2004). *Emotional literacy in the middle school: A 6-step program to promote social, emotional, and academic learning.* Port Chester, NY: Dude.

Meece, D., & Soderman, A. K. (2010). Positive verbal environments: Setting the stage for young children's social development. *Young Children, 65*(5), 81–86.

Mezzacappa, E. (2004). Alerting, orienting, and executive attention: Developmental properties and sociodemographic correlates in an epidemiological sample of young, urban children. *Child Development, 75*(5), 1373–1386.

National Association for the Education of Young Children. (2017). A call for excellence in early childhood education. Retrieved from *www.naeyc.org/policy/excellence.*

National Scientific Council on the Developing Child. (2004). Young children develop in an environment of relationships (Working Paper No. 1). Retrieved from *www.developingchild.net.*

Neuman, S., & Cunningham, L. (2009). The impact of professional development and coaching on early language and literacy instructional practices. *American Education Research Journal, 46*(2), 532–566.

Neuman, S., & Wright, T. (2010). Promoting language and literacy development for early childhood educators: A mixed-methods study of coursework and coaching. *The Elementary School Journal, 111*(1), 63–86.

Obradović, J., Shaffer, A., & Masten, A. S. (2012). Risk in developmental psychopathology: Progress and future directions. In L. C. Mayes & M. Lewis (Eds.), *The Cambridge handbook of environment of human development: A handbook of theory and measurement* (pp. 35–57). New York: Cambridge University Press.

Pennebaker, J. W., & Smyth, J. (2016). *Opening up by writing it down: The healing power of expressive writing* (3rd ed.). New York: Guilford Press.

Phillips, D. (2016). Stability, security, and social dynamics in early childhood environments. In N. K. Lesaux & S. M. Jones (Eds.), *The leading edge of early childhood education: Linking science to policy for a new generation* (pp. 7–28). Cambridge, MA: Harvard Education Press.

Piaget, J. (1952). *The origins of intelligence in children* (M. T. Cook, Trans.). New York: International Universities Press.

Pianta, R. C. (2003). *Experiences in P–3 classrooms: The implications of observational research for redesigning early education.* New York: Foundation for Child Development.

Porges S. W., Doussard-Roosevelt, J. A., & Maiti, A. K. (1994). Vagal tone and the physiological regulation of emotion. *Monographs of the Society for Research in Child Development, 59*(2–3), 167–186.

Rath, T., Reckmeyer, M., & Manning, M. (2009). *How full is your bucket?: For kids.* New York: Gallup Press.

Raver, C. C., Garner, P., & Smith-Donald, R. (2007). The roles of emotion regulation and emotion knowledge for children's academic readiness: Are the links causal? In R. C. Pianta, M. J. Cox, & K. L. Snow (Eds.), *School readiness and the transition to kindergarten in the era of accountability* (pp. 121–147). Baltimore: Brookes.

Raver, C. C., Jones, S. M., Li-Grining, C., Zhai, F., Metzger, M. W., & Solomon, B. (2009). Targeting children's behavior problems in preschool classrooms: A cluster-randomized controlled trial. *Journal of Consulting and Clinical Psychology, 77*(2), 302–316.

Richardson, J. (1999). *Norms put the "Golden Rule" into practice for groups.* Oxford, OH: National Staff Development Council.

Roeser, R. W., Skinner, E., Beers, J., & Jennings, P. A. (2012). Mindfulness training and teachers' professional development: An emerging area of research and practice. *Child Development Perspectives, 6,* 167–173.

Sheridan, S. M., Edwards, C. P., Marvin, C. A., & Knoche, L. L. (2009). Professional development in early childhood programs: Process issues and research needs. *Early Education and Development, 20*(3), 377–401.

Supovitz, J. A. (2002). Developing communities of instructional practice. *Teachers College Record, 104*(8), 1591–1626.

Tschannen-Moran, M., & McMaster, P. (2009). Sources of self-efficacy: Four professional development formats and their relationship to self-efficacy and implementation of a new teaching strategy. *Elementary School Journal, 110*(2), 228–245.

U.S. Department of Education. (2015). *A matter of equity: Preschool in America.* Retrieved from *www2.ed.gov/documents/early-learning/matter-equity-preschool-america.pdf.*

Vail, R., & Heo, Y. (2005). *Sometimes I'm bombaloo.* New York: Scholastic.

Vescio, V., Ross, D., & Adams, A. (2008). A review of research on the impact of professional learning communities on teaching practice and student learning. *Teaching and Teacher Education, 24*(1), 80–91.

Vygotsky, L. (1978). Interaction between learning and development. In M. Gauvain & M. Cole (Eds.), *Readings on the development of children* (pp. 34–40). New York: Scientific American Books.

Yolen, J. (2007). *How do dinosaurs go to school?* New York: Blue Sky Press.

Yoshikawa, H., Weiland, C., Brooks-Gunn, J., Burchinal, M. R., Espinosa, L. M., Gormley, W. T., et al. (2013). Investing in our future: The evidence base for preschool education. Retrieved from *www.fcd-us.org/the-evidence-base-on-preschool.*

Zaslow, M., Martinez-Beck, I., Tout, K., & Halle, T. (2011). *Quality measurement in early childhood settings.* Baltimore: Brookes.

Zaslow, M., Tout, K., Halle, T., Whittaker, J. V., & Lavelle, B. (2010). *Toward the identification of features of effective professional development for early childhood educators: Literature review.* Washington, DC: U.S. Department of Education, Office of Planning, Evaluation and Policy Development, Policy and Program Studies Service.

Zelazo, P. D., & Carlson, S. M. (2012). Hot and cool executive function in childhood and adolescence: Development and plasticity. *Child Development Perspectives, 6*(4), 354–360.

Index

Note. *f* or *t* following a page number indicates a figure or a table.